CHANGING THE LENS

CHANGING THE LENS

EXPLORING THE DEPTHS OF FILM AND PHILOSOPHY

Edited by
**Dr Ruplekha Khullar
Sulagna Pal**

DECLARATION

This is to certify that this volume 'The Philosophy of Film and Film as an Art Form: Teaching Film Appreciation', is an outcome of the research project on art and film appreciation undertaken by the Department of Philosophy, Janki Devi Memorial College, University of Delhi, India. This volume has been edited by Dr Ruplekha Khullar and Ms Sulagna Pal who hereby declare that this work is original and has not been submitted elsewhere for publication.

Dr Ruplekha Khullar
Sulagna Pal

Published by
Renu Kaul Verma
Vitasta Publishing Pvt Ltd
4348/4C, Ansari Road, Daryaganj
New Delhi - 110 002
info@vitastapublishing.com

ISBN: 978-81-19670-94-9
© Vitasta Publishing
First Edition 2024
MRP ₹495

All Rights Reserved.
No part of this publication may be reproduced, stored in a retrieval system, or transmitted in any form, or by any means–electronic, mechanical, photocopying, recording or otherwise–without the prior permission of the publisher. Opinions expressed in this book are the author's own. The publisher is in no way responsible for these.

Edited by Anuradha Mukherjee
Typeset & Cover Design by Somesh Kumar Mishra
Printed by Vikas Computer and Printers, New Delhi

CONTENT

Acknowledgements ix

Introduction xiii

Chapter 1   A Guide to Philosophising Cinema   1

Chapter 2   The Retelling of Mughal-e-Azam   20

Chapter 3   Film and Culture   33

Chapter 4   The Resurgence of Film   51

Chapter 5   Cinematic Reflections on Reality   69

Chapter 6   Deciphering the Unknown   98

Chapter 7   Painting Gandhi on the Celluloid Canvas   128

Endnotes 159

ACKNOWLEDGEMENTS

This volume on Film Appreciation is a collaborative venture of the members of the Department of Philosophy, Janki Devi Memorial College, University of Delhi. It seeks to fulfil the perceived need of undergraduate students to have a basic understanding of the subject of film appreciation within a philosophy curriculum. The volume was a stipulated outcome of the proceedings of the Symposium on Art and Film Appreciation which was held in late 2018 as part of the student-faculty research project undertaken by the department. The primary intention and ultimate goal of the symposium was to gather material to compose a single work that could function as a text and act as an important reference for students and undergraduate scholars working in this field.

    The volume contains the work of students and teachers, related to topics in the prescribed course, as well as expositions of presentations made by various filmmakers and academicians during the symposium. The task of facilitating student research work and mentoring them, organising the symposium, recording and transcribing lectures and the final writing of the volume has been accomplished from start to finish by the joint efforts of the teachers of the department, namely, Dr Ruplekha Khullar, Ms Himanshu Bala Jagatdeb, Dr Sudnya Kulkarni, Dr Jayanti Sahoo (who also presented a paper, *A Post-modern Analysis of Continuity and Change in Indian Cinema*, at one session of the symposium), Dr Sipu Jayswal, Dr Rahul Maurya (who has since moved to the Department of Philosophy and Religion at BHU), Dr Vel Murugan, and Ms Sulagna Pal.

We wish to acknowledge with gratitude the many people who have made it possible for us to produce this volume.

We are indebted to all our speakers who so graciously shared their years of work experience as filmmakers, critics, and academics through their lectures at the symposium. We were fortunate to have amongst us Professor V. Sanil, Professor of Philosophy at the Department of Humanities and Social Sciences, Indian Institute of Technology, Delhi as our Keynote Speaker; Dr Soumyabrat Choudhury, Associate Professor, Arts & Aesthetics, JNU; Professor Vebhuti Duggal, School of Culture & Creative Expressions, Ambedkar University; Ms Vani Subramanian, Documentary Film Maker and Feminist Activist; Ms Mahiema Anand, Filmmaker, Storyteller, and Writer; Ms Anandana Kapoor, Film and Art Director, Communication Paradigms and Film Studies, Jamia Milia Islamia; and Mr Sudipto Sen, Independent Filmmaker and Cinema Academic. Their lectures and interactions with the audience raised the bar of discussion to a very high level for both teachers and students present at the symposium.

We owe our gratitude to Dr Sudarsan Dash of USIEF, Delhi, for his invaluable support and guidance that helped us approach speakers who were experts and had long-term associations with the field of cinema. Dr Dash has always been our go-to person for any seminar, conference, or symposium that the department has organised, and it would have been impossible to have so many successful events at the Philosophy department of JDMC without his help.

This work would not have seen the light of day without the aid and encouragement from the Principal of Janki Devi Memorial College, Prof Swati Pal. We owe our gratitude and thanks to her for extending all possible logistical support for the symposium, from sanctioning grants for the students' research work to agreeing so enthusiastically to present a very absorbing lecture at the symposium on the 'Villains of Bollywood', and for providing help and encouragement in every other way.

Our students team, Athira Naick, Surbhi Singh, Karuna Jha, Ruchika Khavadiya, Gautami Jain, and Chavi Joshi are to be congratulated for putting in a concerted effort to collect information from various sources and following it up with necessary research and then jointly writing the chapter on *Films on Gandhi*.

Thanks are due to Yamini and Shruti, students of the third year class of 2019 for arranging the videography of the symposium sessions. Thanks, are also owed to all the students of the philosophy department who were involved in some form or the other in the successful organisation of the symposium.

We would like to express our gratitude to the college administrative staff as we could not have moved an inch without their help and cooperation. Mr Avinash was always there to resolve any glitches with the microphones or projector in the Seminar room. A special mention must be made of Mr Surender Kumar of the Office, who in his usual business-like yet reassuring manner, oversaw every arrangement with smooth efficiency.

INTRODUCTION

FORMAL education which centres around classroom teaching, textbooks, information gathering, and examinations, aims at certain standard learning outcomes—intellectual development, knowledge gain, skill acquisition, and preparations for earning a livelihood. However, formal education allows little scope for self-exploration, innovation, or the dynamic experience of sharing knowledge. It is thus not a means suited for instilling other life-sustaining values that allow a person to grow to their full potential. It is powerless in helping people cultivate their sensibilities or reform their attitudes, nor helpful in acquiring a sense of identity and finding cultural roots—all of which are integral to stable mental health. Art fosters good energy. It provides creative satisfaction and is a great mode of finding solace and comfort. It makes the youth deeply appreciative of the positive aspects of life and sensitises them towards other humans. This sensitivity in turn helps young people hone their interpersonal skills and organise their behavioural responses in a balanced manner. They experience an immediate sense of bonding and oneness not only with other people but with their surroundings as well. Finally, art can stimulate the powers of concentration.

Art forms are varied and difficult to capture within the academic realm. The experience and appreciation of a work of art are also, in an important sense, purely subjective experiences unique to a beholder of art, and do not lend themselves to easy analysis.

Yet a painting or sculpture may find a way into the consciousness of a beholder because of the cultural connections it has with aspects of their life even though they may have had little exposure to the visual arts. That said, a study of art history and the history of an art form (however rudimentary), in addition to some knowledge of the elements, the medium, and the methods used in the creative process, go a long way in helping students develop an understanding of art in all its forms. The basic steps in the process of understanding and interpreting art involve the following:

- An objective description of the work of art, its formal structure, and physical attributes
- A subjective analysis combining the above with one's emotional response to the work
- An understanding of socio-cultural context, including information about the period in which a particular work of art was created, the local or geographical environment, information about religious practices associated with it, and the personal history of the artist
- Excavating meaning based on the above knowledge
- A critical evaluation of the artwork for its aesthetic or cultural value

The process also applies to understanding film as art.

Cinema is a unique form of art. Indeed, the question of how the film is to be counted as an art form is a subject of much academic debate. According to *Cahiers du Cinema* co-founder Andre Bazin, cinema is not at par with painting or theatre because cinema has attributes of a documentary and is not pure creation. Poetry, painting, and theatre work under different aesthetic principles and functional cultures. They also have a different audience. In a way, cinema is superior to painting and photography. It represents reality differently and more truly without taking liberties.[1]

One finds a course in 'Art and Film Appreciation' or 'Art and Film Studies' in the curricula of most universities, included usually as part of the syllabus of Philosophy or Literature programs offered at both honours and program levels. Such courses are designed to promote a unique, independent, and honest perception of aesthetic and moral values, sharpening the student's sensibilities through the experience of art and cinema. They foster the courage and confidence to express one's opinions, explore the inner self through symbolic associations, integrate varied ideas, and develop empathy towards others and nature.

The teacher of a course on Art and Film finds it a challenge to teach the subject without specific texts outlined for the same. This volume was planned around one-half of the course, namely *Film Appreciation*. The intention behind the exercise was to produce a single work comprising some important aspects of the subject of film studies that could prove to be a valuable teaching source for the same. On completing a course in film appreciation, students are expected to be able to interpret cinematic works, understand the processes involved in the cinematic expression of political, social, and cultural ideas as well as aesthetic values, and understand the role and impact of films on the history and cultures of the world.

Viewing a film from a layman's perspective can simply mean that it is nothing more than yet another source of entertainment. A more involved audience might have a richer experience noticing and appreciating the intricacies of light, camera angle, music, story, and narrative style. But a teacher must go beyond these experiences and analyse cinema's strengths as a medium of instruction that can be used to educate people about an entire spectrum of issues ranging between political, social, historical, economic, and cultural. They must investigate the horsepower cinema has as a vehicle, onboard which the viewer can travel across periods and eras, across galaxies and universes, and the expanse of the minds of humans. A film can be beautifully fragmented, tantalizingly exposing discrete elements scattered across the audience's vision, or it can present a fine blend of these elements to craft a narrative about literally anything under the sun—complex interpersonal relationships amongst people from myriad cultures or social mores, customs, and practices—the list is infinite. Filmmakers can be engaging storytellers or powerful influencers guiding the naïve mind into uncharted territories.

A film analyst unpacks the complex cinematic experience of a viewer. Much depends on who the audience is. Different genres attract different viewers. A casual watcher will only look for diversions, not paying any attention to a film's finer nuances. Films for mass entertainment are focused simply on providing titillation and 'time-pass' entertainment, and the filmmaker can often get away by doing shoddy and careless work. Biographies on the lives of well-known and not-so-well-known historical personas are much more carefully designed and are well-received by a certain kind of audience. Viewers are allowed an intimate look into the real-life experiences of the protagonist who may be a person of interest to them.

Crime and suspense thrillers are fascinating to an inquisitive mind. Horror films surpass all other genres in arousing fear and terror, which can be extremely pleasurable emotions when one is secure in the knowledge that it's all happening only on screen.

However, no matter how niche the audience a film intends to draw to itself, there is usually a twofold incentive for a filmmaker: creating a lasting impression on the people who watch their film and reaching out to as wide an audience as possible. This longevity of impact, especially on a common population, is what many directors aspire to. Successful directors attain it with a few of their films. Reaching out to the common man remains a motto for every filmmaker, and failing to do so leaves them with a sense of being unfulfilled.

There are different streams within the academic study of Cinema; each with a distinct approach to the subject. Film studies, film theory, film appreciation, and philosophy of film are overlapping approaches to the theoretical exploration of films as an art form that is simultaneously a medium of education, a vehicle for the dissemination of information and values, and a means of political message-making. Understanding and appreciation of this art form comes from exposure, not only to films and works of art but to the theory behind the field as well. Besides that, no student of film can conduct a fair evaluation without at least some knowledge of the empirical tools of film craft. Knowledge thus fortified will enable students to develop a critical perspective on the subject.

The philosophy of film is an independent sub-field of the philosophy of art and aesthetics. It aims at in-depth analysis of the deeper issues regarding the nature and purpose of films, their exegesis, and the cinematic experience as a unique aesthetic experience. How is the philosophy of film different from film theory? Despite obvious overlaps, the philosophy of film differs from film theory in that the latter is more about a technical exposé of cinema, its genres, its specialised paraphernalia, its authorship, and its style, while the former ideally would apply abstract philosophical concepts while examining the medium, its technicalities, its value as entertainment, its aesthetics, or its power to inculcate morality.

It is important to understand that the philosophy of films did not have the assertive power at the time of its inception around the 1920s, which it has now. Philosophers were hesitant to be counted amongst the few in academia who tried to bring cinema under the rubric of art forms. According to the Stanford Encyclopaedia of Philosophy (SEP),

> Because the study of film is already institutionalised within academia in the discipline of film studies, and because that field includes a separate sub-field of film theory, it might seem that, unlike literature and music,

say, the film is already well-served by this institutional base. From this point of view, the philosophy of film is redundant, occupying a space that has already been carved out by an alternative discipline...[2]

Henri Bergson was perhaps the first philosopher to make an impact on film studies with his book *Creative Evolution* in 1907. Bergson described Cinema as 'moving images' and a 'cinematographic mechanism' used by the intellect to perceive reality in its totality. Though Bergson did not write much about film theory per se, or make it his chief concern, his ideas on the power of 'intuition' in the holistic grasp of reality and his notion of time or 'duration' became an important part of the framework of understanding film in recent times. His legacy can be seen in the works of French philosophers Giles Deleuze and Jean-Louis Schefer, and other well-known philosophers of film such as Andrei Tarkovsky and Andre Bazin.

The discipline has gained stature since then. Cinema on its own contributes majorly towards humanity's understanding of life and culture. But to take its place as an art form alongside other traditional art forms such as theatre, dance, and painting, each of which contributes to enhancing this understanding in their own unique ways, cinema had to be explored for its aesthetic functionality and philosophers found it incumbent to give it an academic grounding. Over time, the philosophy of films became a pertinent area of interest for researchers in the field of art and aesthetics, and a prominent subject for philosophical reflection.

Troubles arose when the philosophy of films was

separated from film studies, thus going against what was well-accepted in an institutionalised sense. Sub-fields of film theory within film studies have been dominated by a wide range of theoretical commitments that many Anglo-American philosophers did not share. Such philosophers, therefore, thought to make minor revisions within the sub-fields rather than beginning a new line of research into films that would avoid the problematic assumptions of film theory. This, along with the exploration of film as a legitimate topic within aesthetics, led to the development of a philosophically informed mode of thinking about films. Philosophers today are concerned with issues related to how the philosophy of film should be constituted as an autonomous field of study both within aesthetics and independently.

According to SEP (The Stanford Encyclopaedia of Philosophy),

> What role is there for film interpretation in the field? How do studies of particular films relate to more theoretical studies of the medium as such? What about philosophy in film, a popular mode of philosophic thinking about film? Is there a unified model that can be employed to characterize this newly vitalized domain of philosophic inquiry?[3]

This volume does not intend to justify the interest of philosophers in films, which is a given. Instead, it seeks to explain and highlight the main points of this interest by taking a close look at selective genres and important historical movements that impacted the way films were made. It explores some of the tools of the trade and attempts to establish significant parallels between cinema and other art forms, reiterating cinema's essentially artistic nature. At every step, it seeks to point out problem areas critical to the discussion of cinema. In all of this, it roughly follows the direction taken by the Symposium in its sessions.

The book initiates a profound exploration of the interconnected realms of philosophy and film, transcending cinema's conventional role as mere entertainment. Professor V. Sanil's opening chapter underscores the evolution of philosophy into an intellectual meta-discipline with a keen interest in cinema, viewing films not only for amusement but as objects of academic scrutiny.

Chapter 2, written by Professor Soumyabrat Choudhry, meticulously unravels the nuanced layers of meaning beneath Madhubala's portrayal in 'Mughal-e-Azam.' Subsequent chapters navigate linguistic and non-verbal modes of communication, delve into the revolutionary French New Wave, and explore Cinematic Realism's objective portrayal of reality. The book scrutinises documentary filmmaking as a non-fictional, socially impactful medium, shedding light on its potential to inform, educate, and motivate societal change. This sequential academic journey interweaves philosophy, cultural communication, cinematic movements, and documentary filmmaking, presenting a comprehensive understanding of cinema's diverse dimensions. The last chapter is the product of students' research and was written by the students of Philosophy at Janki Devi Memorial College.

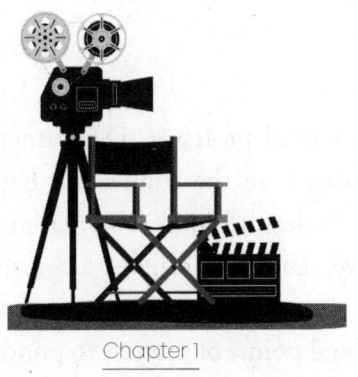

Chapter 1

A Guide to Philosophising Cinema
by Professor V. Sanil

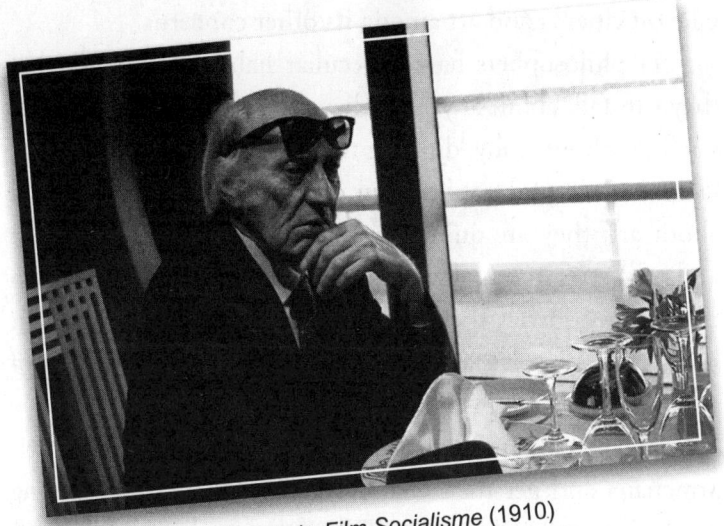

Fig.1 Badiou in *Film Socialisme* (1910)

V. SANIL, a retired professor, Department of Philosophy, IIT Delhi, focuses on the connection between philosophy and cinema. Professor Sanil's observations are concise yet comprehensive, and his insights are acute and nuanced. He presents an excellent summation of the theme, while providing several points of interest to ponder upon.

He expresses his delight at philosophers taking an interest in cinema. As researchers and professionals, scholars in philosophy no longer watch films simply as a source of entertainment, but as objects of academic interest. Philosophy has thus become an intellectual meta-discipline that has a take on cinema and art among its other concerns.

Yet philosophers have a peculiar habit of thinking that they can talk about anything they wish sitting on their lofty perch, without really 'dirtying their hands'. The unfortunate fact is, while philosophers can develop philosophies of and about art, they are quite often unable to appreciate the art and aesthetics in actual works of art displayed, for instance, in exhibitions; just as they philosophise about science without being able to solve a differential equation. 'Philosophy of science is to science what ornithology is to birds.'

Sanil is convinced that philosophers must get off their armchairs and get their feet wet at least once by becoming filmmakers and making films if they are to understand the craft or construct meaningful theory around it. They have at their command the tools that can nourish the art of filmmaking by introducing new ways of using age-old filmmaking techniques. When a philosopher becomes a filmmaker using his own tools alongside those of the craft, he succeeds in applying himself meaningfully to the subject under study.

We should learn a thing or two from the great philosophers of the past. Greek philosophers engaged with their subject intimately, cutting deep across lines of pre-set understandings. They were not ones to stand at the door and peep in. Plato, despite being a philosopher by calling, was so inspired by Pythagoras that he made science and mathematics the central disciplines to be taught at the academy he started in Athens, in 387 BCE. So insistent was he that every student of philosophy study these subjects thoroughly that he had the following line inscribed at the entrance of the academy, 'Let none but geometers enter through this door'.

Descartes and Kant who wrote on the philosophy of mathematics, developed mathematical concepts, axioms, theorems, and proofs. Kant actively engaged in conceptualising the entire discipline of mathematics and Descartes started a separate discipline called analytic geometry. Hegel delved into the field of Greek mathematics, especially calculus, though, in retrospect, Hegel's views had appeared naïve and unstructured and were swept aside by more sophisticated systems.

It helps to keep in mind that much work, be it in any area, can remain unacknowledged unless the right circumstances present themselves. Consider Albert Einstein, whose name today is synonymous with the general theory of relativity. The curious fact is that Einstein's work on relativity went unrewarded in 1915, as the Nobel Committee held that relativity was an unproven theory. Instead, Einstein received the Nobel Prize for his discovery of the law of the photoelectric effect, which he had published much earlier, in 1905. Thus, unhappy circumstances led to the incredible truth that a Nobel Prize for one of the most important theories of all times was never awarded. This should be a fair warning that the lines of research need to be traced clearly, all work documented carefully, and the horizons of philosophy pushed beyond their boundaries to engage intimately with creative processes outside the usual realm of philosophical debate. Professor Sanil calls this 'getting passionate' about a subject.

Getting passionate about cinema can be an extremely rewarding experience. Back in 2013, French Philosopher Alain Badiou, who translated the latest version of Plato's Republic, wrote extensively about cinema and followed it up by planning a film on the renowned philosopher. Writing the screenplay for *The Life of Plato*, he thought of casting Brad Pitt as Plato, Meryl Streep as Plato's wife, and Sean Connery as the great Socrates. Badiou is reported to have said that he wanted to 'bring Plato, emblem of universal wisdom, to the contemporary temple of commercial images, the propaganda machine of American life, the capital of the capitalist corruption, Hollywood!'[1]

Badiou even acted in a film, a fleeting cameo in Jean Luc Godard's *Film Socialisme* (1910), in which Badiou is shown as himself, writing at his desk. In his inimitable style, Badiou says in one of his articles, 'I've never before seen images of myself in which I am so much myself!'

Closer to home, Sanil points to Indian writer and philosopher Ramchandra Guha, who choreographed and presented several simple dance pieces which, even though not technically great pieces, managed to instil meaning into the movements and fuse soul and body together through dance.

On a different note, Sanil elaborates on Plato's cave allegory to explain how philosophers proposed the idea of motion pictures much before cinema was invented. Plato understood that humankind may in general be capable of thought and speech, but it had little or no understanding of the realm of forms. Plato, therefore, used the power of moving images to convey allegorically the idea of forms.

> Plato likens people untutored in the Theory of Forms to prisoners chained in a cave, unable to turn their heads. All they can see is the wall of the cave. Behind them burns a fire. Between the fire and the prisoners, there is a parapet, along which puppeteers can walk. The puppeteers, who are behind the prisoners, hold up puppets that cast shadows on the wall of the cave. The prisoners are unable to see these puppets, the real objects that pass behind them. What the prisoners see and hear are shadows and echoes cast by objects that they do not see.[2]

Knowing nothing of the real objects being paraded behind them, the prisoners consider the shadows they see on the wall as real. If they could discuss their experiences with one another, they would use names and words to refer to these shadows and not to the real things.

In Plato's analogy, we see what happens when a prisoner escapes his chains and ventures outside the cave into the bright sunlight. At first, the prisoner is blinded by the sun and wants to rush back into the comfort of familiar surroundings within the cave. As his eyes adjust to the glare, he sees things and recognises them for what they, in fact, are. He realises the extent of his ignorance. The Sun here refers to the 'Idea' or the realm of forms. The escaped prisoner is the philosopher. He has his eyes now trained on the sun but wishes to go back inside and enlighten his companions and free them from their ignorance.

However, when he reenters the dim environs of the cave, his eyes that have looked at the dazzling sun outside cannot now see anything inside distinctly. He must wait awhile for them to adjust to the reduced lighting. In the meantime, he has come to realise that he must tread carefully as the ignorant are in large numbers and are reluctant to have their eyes opened by someone who has fled from their midst. The ignorant are the common people who have trusted the shadowy images (of objects) that they have been looking at all along. They are not to be easily persuaded by the philosopher who has looked upon the sun and is now exhorting them to trust the so-called truth revealed in its light. The lesson Plato wishes to impart is simple. Realising the truth does not come easily, but in its pursuit, the mind breaks free from the chains of collective ignorance and recognises the Idea, the 'universal' under which all particulars of experience are subsumed.

It is just such a miracle that is wrought by a philosophy class on students after the first few lectures, says Sanil. They are confused up until the discovery that they had mistaken the shadows to be real and have only now learned what reality is.

The allegory of the cave may be seen as a reflection of the history of cinema's invention. The human situation is similar to the common man watching a film in the screening room of a theatre, and taking whatever he sees as objective reality. What happens on celluloid is akin to the illusory world depicted on the walls of the cave, but a philosopher must get out of the theatre and confront the real world outside.

Cinema is not simply shadows – it is an art as well as a mode of thinking truth. According to Badiou, the task of philosophy, difficult as it may seem, is to reconfigure truth into cinema.

In his book, *Philosophy & Cinema*, Badiou explains what happens to Plato's allegory if looked at through the lens of current times. The prisoner emerges from the underground cave which Badiou likens to a screening room, only to find a world in which truth has become indistinguishable from manufactured opinion. In a postmodern world, Plato's allegory is 'overturned' and we find ourselves in a world where half-truths, relative truths, and illusions prevail–a world of free market economies, mindless consumerism, and carefully constituted 'truths'. Badiou's project is to explain the role of cinema in depicting and shaping the drama and spectacle of social reality. He aims to rethink cinema, in what he calls the 'recommencement of philosophy' through a return to Plato. Today, philosophy is being requisitioned by cinema as much as it itself requisitions cinema; there is not only a philosophy of cinema but also *philosophy as cinema*.

Is Cinema an Art Form?

A familiar way in which philosophers talk about cinema is to discuss the aesthetics of film. Aesthetics as a formal branch of philosophy takes it upon itself to settle, amongst other things, the question, 'What is art?' A definition sets rules and draws boundaries around an object of art and makes it what it is. Yet no sooner than it does so, an artist will come along and make an artwork that violates some of the rules. The thing is, *art* can never be circumscribed by its definition. It breaks out of its boundaries all too often. So, what can one make of questions such as *what kind of an art form is cinema?*

    Firstly, it is a challenge to fit cinema into the mould of well-defined art forms such as dance, music, or painting. The latter work under different aesthetic principles and have different audiences; they serve different cultural functions. Cinema is not a purely human creation in the sense that, unlike other art forms, there is technology at the core of cinema. A film artist does not need or use technology in the same way as a musician needs and uses a guitar, or a painter uses a brush. The nature of the moving image is inextricably tied to the fact that it is technologically produced, though the attempt is to imitate life in such a manner as to make the technological rendering of 'facts' undiscernible. Secondly, cinema uses technology to produce pomp and show! It 'dresses' the truth—embellishes it with special effects. Using artificial rain to heighten romance in a scene is a cliched but typical example. Sanil discusses the fascinating ways in which films depend on technology to display their art and how studying the industrial aspects of cinema could give one a fresh perspective on it.

The fact that technology makes up such an integral part of films is the reason why the people associated with filmmaking–the producers, directors, actors, and of course the technicians–refer to their profession, not as an art, but as an industry. That is the way it is. 'Cinema is an industry whether you wish to accept it or not.' Whether one is speaking of art cinema or commercial cinema, as one of the great directors put it, 'cinema ends when the capital ends'. You need the capital because without money you cannot make cinema.

A third challenge to cinema being art is that it does not require a connoisseur to appreciate its worth. If anything, cinema is a mass art–produced for the masses by mass technology. People from different socio-cultural backgrounds watch cinema. Films address these different audiences and connect with them in different ways; therefore the distinction between popular cinema and art cinema. There is an ongoing debate about mass art, whether it is art at all since the only thing that defines it is the fact that it is consumed by different social classes–a fact that also compromises its status as art. Even though people like Noel Carroll have argued that mass art does display characteristic structural features that can place it in the same realm as high art, elevating all sorts of cinema to the level of artwork is, to say the least, problematic.[3] Because of its monetary, technological, and mass consumption aspects, cinema is considered a very impure art.

Philosophy of Films as a Subject

Filmmakers often resist the making of films into a subject for academic study. An analytical philosophical approach to the study of culture in general, and cinema in particular, avoids the active dynamics between the cinemagoer and the film—what has been referred to as the cinematic or contextual imaginary. In this context, Sanil echoes the views of a group of film scholars including Noel Carrol, David Bordwell, and Clive Meyer, whose arguments oppose the views of the likes of French philosopher Giles Deleuze and psychoanalyst Felix Guattari. The latter created new concepts and terms and devised unique new ways of using existing philosophical concepts to discuss cinema.[4] Meaningful discussions of cinema, in the views of Deleuze and Guattari, could take place within the overarching philosophical frameworks and theories about society, culture, language, history, and the human psyche, offered for instance, by Freudian and Lacanian Psychoanalysis, Structuralism, Post-structuralism, and Marxism—what Bordwell aggregates as Grand Theory.

According to Deleuze and Guattari, cinema 'thinks'; cinema has the conceptual power to philosophise. For Bordwell et al. such grand conceptual frameworks can neither capture in entirety the complex nuances of the 'cinema event',[5] nor give an entirely satisfactory explanation of the viewers' emotional involvement with a film or its impact on society in general. Their complaint about the producers of grand theory, as Bordwell puts it, is that,

> Rather than formulating a question, posing a problem, or trying to come to grips with an intriguing film, the writer often takes as the central task, the proving of a theoretical position by adducing films as examples. From the theory, the writer moves to a particular

case. Lévi-Straussian analysis of the Western, feminist conceptions of the body in film, Jamesonian accounts of the postmodernity of *Blade Runner*—again and again, research is seen chiefly as 'applying' a theory to a particular film or historical period.[6]

The film is about how it affects viewer sensibilities; it is about the wide variety of viewing and listening practices. In *Critical Cinema: Beyond the Theory of Practice* (2011), Clive Meyer suggests that viewing cinema is a different experience from watching a 'movie' at home or visiting an art gallery. He argues for film theorists to re-engage with the specificity of philosophical concepts in discussing cinema as a medium distinct from others. Writers such as these, advocate for theories instead of Theories, the difference being that theories in the lower case, allow local flavours to emerge.

The problem in searching for a unified theory that will apply to films in general, is that one no longer focuses on the totality of the experience of cinema, grasping only at the philosophical aspects as a tool for understanding cinema. This approach leads, at best, only to an imperfect understanding of the power of cinema. The wonderfully funny 1966 Italian film, *Uccellaccie Uccellini*, The Hawks and the Sparrows, by Pier Paolo Pasolini, is a case in point. The film is an allegorical tale about a comical, Charlie Chaplin-like father and his good-natured but goofy son, who undertake a journey together, accompanied by a philosophical talking crow who represents the quirks and confusions of life. Not many people could fathom exactly what Pasolini intended to show in his film; perhaps about how there are all kinds of people in the world, those who prey on others and those who are preyed upon–hawks and sparrows. Yet the film delighted the audiences with its warm, amusing, compassionate, and yet intellectually oblique musings on politics, religion, and life in general, superbly portrayed by one of Italy's greatest clowns, Toto, playing the father, and Ninetto Davoli, his son. Yet, due to its overt engagement with the doctrines of Christianity, and the Marxist themes of poverty and class struggle, the film has been reduced to no more than a reference point in empirical film studies.

The thing is, many of the critical elements of cinema, including light, sound, music, camera angles, and mood, are superfluous for philosophical purposes. Anglo-American psychoanalytical philosophers focused exclusively on what happened in films and the nature of the emotional involvement of the spectator. Advocates of cognitive philosophy, Richard Allen and Murray Smith *Film Theory & Philosophy*, eds., 1997, found that cinema revealed interesting facts about our cognitive abilities. Connecting knowledge with the emotional responses of the audience, they enquired about what could be learned regarding our cognitive mechanism that helps us respond to things like horror, melodrama, etc. Thus, cinema came to be used as a methodological tool to 'do philosophy'. Ingmar Bergman's *The Seventh Seal* (1957), for instance, would be screened to initiate discussion on hell, death, or existence; or *The Matrix* (1999) to explain the relationship between realms or versions of 'reality'; all the while deliberately ignoring its cinematic elements in the effort to paraphrase the film. With Anglo-American

Analytical philosophy's rapidly developing interest in cinema around the 1980s, the philosophy of film had come to be firmly established as a sub-domain of the philosophy of art.

Today, there is an ongoing debate between critics who hold cinema to be incapable of being anything more than a pedagogic tool to teach philosophy, and scholars of film study who see it as a source of knowledge, believing in cinema's capacity to 'do philosophy', contributing to philosophy itself by raising and generating debate on critical issues and helping to develop abilities and attitudes.

Early philosophers were concerned with maintaining exclusivity for their domain and dismissed the arts with disdain as being merely poor aspirers of philosophy's lofty power to depict truth. Cinema as an art form dealt with moving images while philosophy's business was thinking. For Platonists, image was a great enemy of thought. For Descartes, the human subject beheld the world from a distance and claimed certainty only for thought. In sharp contrast, Sanil points to the works of Stanley Cavell and Stephen Mulhall who, inspired by Einstein and Heidegger, substantiate an opposite view.

Heidegger denied the conception of the individual human being as a thinking subject standing apart from the world in cognitive isolation. His Dasein was 'in the world', inextricably caught up in it. Philosophical thinking in the Heideggerian sense is not some sort of artificial thinking distinct from life, providing fixed meanings to things. Heidegger said we humans are already a problem for ourselves as we constantly bicker about who can and cannot do philosophy.

Cavell eschews theory on the grounds that it puts artificial constraints on finding meaning. Philosophy of film can deliver gainful insights about many topics of general concern without becoming a sort of meta-discipline that studies cinema from a distance and in terms of a privileged set of abstract concepts and theories.

Cavell and Mulhall say cinema is itself a mode of philosophical thinking. We do not need to paraphrase a film; we do not have to create a higher-order theory about what cinema does; cinema is already thinking. It teaches you how to consider its subject matter. Philosophers think with concepts, science thinks with functional relations, and cinematographers think with images. Cinema is thinking in action. Heidegger gestured towards understanding the existential meaning of the 'film event' which theoretical concepts tended to block out. It would require attending to the malleability of sounds and rhythms rather than objects or concepts with fixed meanings.

For Cavell, philosophy is intrinsically concerned with scepticism. Cavell (1971) calls films 'the moving image of scepticism' in his book *The World Viewed: Reflections on the Ontology of Film*. To understand the depth of what Cavell means by this statement, one would need to go into an examination of his idea of 'acknowledgement' with film and unravel its implications, which takes us beyond the scope of Sanil's presentation. He, however, explains broadly that here, Cavell is referring to a sort of Cartesian scepticism about the existence of an external world. Just as the sceptic doubts whether anything is real or understands that he is required to consider things to be real even though they may be mere figments of our imagination, so also, the viewer sees the world depicted on screen as an unreal world from which they are distanced by time and place, and yet must take it as it is presented–take it as real. With human knowledge being potentially incomplete and imperfect, we have a lack of conviction and are sceptical about our relation with external nature–with reality. Our inability to 'know' completely and nature's reluctance to reveal herself puts us in a condition in which we know as real what does not count as reality. This is true of the film too. Cavell has argued that as film shares this issue with philosophy, it can provide philosophic insights on its own; it can help build a better understanding of things, which can save us from the inherent scepticism underlying human existence.

Cavell considers scepticism endemic not just to philosophy but to all aspects of modern culture, including literature, politics, psychoanalysis, and cinema. Cinema shows us the inadequacies of the grand theories of systematic philosophy. They are not what help cinema capture meaning; rather it is the cinematic technological aspects such as image and sound that help it to do so. There is, of course, a counterview that looks upon the storytelling character of fiction films as a hindrance on the path to getting counted amongst films genuinely being on or doing philosophy. In his book *Pursuits of Happiness: The Hollywood Comedy of Remarriage,* Cavell takes up examples of seven very entertaining, and rather offhand movies produced in Hollywood during the 30s and 40s, a series of dialogue-heavy romantic comedies such as *It Happened One Night* (1934), *The Lady Eve* (1941),

The Awful Truth (1937), and *Adam's Rib* (1949), which were based on the highly improbable theme of the screen pair of protagonists reuniting after a string of unfortunate circumstances, misunderstandings, divorce, and separation.[7] Surprisingly, Cavell chooses these films to demonstrate cinema as a serious form of art.

Stephen Mulhall, the other philosopher whom Sanil cites, also argued that films themselves can philosophise. His book *On Film*, went through several editions, the first beginning with a study of the four *Alien* movies, the second expanding its range to include films such as the *Mission: Impossible* series and Steven Spielberg's *Minority Report*, and successive editions including films from science fiction, thrillers and other genres.[8] Mulhall recalls Stanley Cavell's observations on the nature of cinema, occasionally referring to philosophers such as Nietzsche, Heidegger, and Wittgenstein, in an attempt to show how the films in his list do not simply throw up themes that may be of interest to philosophers but display a capacity to build up a body of original philosophical insights around common issues in life, that may help humans cope with them meaningfully. Mulhall gives us a guided design model of philosophy[9] and tells us that these great films aim to give us the tools and skills necessary to deal with life and personal relationships.

Conclusion

Whatever position one may take on the prospect of 'cinematic philosophy,' it may be inferred that the philosophical relevance of film has engaged philosophers over a long period; and even those who deny that films can contribute to philosophy or that philosophers think through films, have had to acknowledge the fact that films endow audiences with access to pertinent philosophical issues and assist in a deeper understanding of things by providing unique conceptual frameworks. This is a big achievement for philosophy itself.[10] It can be comfortably said that both philosophers and filmmakers are placed on the same existential plane in relation to cinema.

Sanil concludes with an important aspect of cinema today—technology. It is very difficult to see cinema without seeing what technology brings to it. The idea of technology is complex. In an obvious way technology is there for human use and consumption; to extend our human abilities and therefore to help us meet our human needs. But there is more to technology than just being an object for human consumption, a mere tool. It cannot be taken for granted for technology has a revolutionary porosity that allows it to anticipate our ways and draws us into its world.

Interestingly, technology was sought to be put in place in 1995, when two experimental directors from Scandinavia, Lars von Trier and Thomas Vinterberg, started a movement for filmmakers called *Dogme 95*. They created the 'Dogme 95 Manifesto'[11] and the 'Vows of Chastity', expressing the following rules for making films that would reflect the traditional values of the film—plot, acting, and theme, and excluding the use of elaborate special effects or technology:
- Shooting must be performed on location, without providing props or sets that do not logically exist within that setting.

- Use diegetic sound only. Sounds must never be produced, such as music that does not exist within the scene.
- All shots must be handheld. Movement, immobility, and stability must be attained by hand, not in post-production.
- The film must be in colour, with no special lighting. If there's not enough exposure, a single lamp may be attached to the camera.
- There can be no optical work or lens filters.
- No 'superficial' action (such as staged murders, elaborate stunts, etc.)
- Geographical alienation is strictly forbidden, meaning the film must take place here and now.
- No identifiable genre
- Academy 35mm is the only accepted film format
- Directors must not be credited.

The accompanying *Vow of Chastity* reads as follows: Furthermore, I swear as a director to refrain from personal taste! I am no longer an artist. I swear to refrain from creating a 'work', as I regard the instant as more important than the whole. My supreme goal is to force the truth out of my characters and settings. I swear to do so by all the means available and at the cost of any good taste and any aesthetic considerations. Thus, I make my VOW OF CHASTITY.[12]

Fellow Danish directors Kristian Levring and Søren Kragh-Jacobsen joined the two philosophers, forming the

'Dogme 95 Collective' or the 'Dogme Brethren' as they came to be known. The movement was purportedly an attempt to reclaim power for the directors as artists, from the studios that wielded it. But those associated with the movement were technological wizards who started filming at the age of thirteen. They were no strangers to technical innovation and used them in their films.

What Sanil meant to say was that these filmmakers too used technology, but in innovative ways that allowed them to claim that they were 'different'; but perhaps they were different simply because they may have had radical, anarchist, or even nudist parents. You become rebellious when you are held captive and cinematographers might strain as captives of cinematic norms and practices. It is from such moments that meaningful cinema of a different kind will emerge.

Take, for instance, the use of 3D which gives us a quasi-human way of looking at reality. 3D technology opens up possibilities for cinema to define a novel cognitive approach to understanding our relatedness to the world.

Just as one can find philosophy in the everyday moments of life or hold on to passing thoughts, one is also able to find philosophy in the tiniest of images captured by the camera.

As Sanil says elsewhere,

> We are led to acknowledge that filmmakers pursue and extend concepts through the practices of film…Philosophy takes cinema as a conceptual practice. This is not to see cinema as an expression of ideas. The task of philosophy is to propose concepts that respond to the inventions and innovations taking place in the history of cinema.[13]

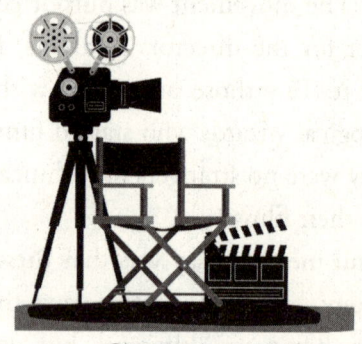

Chapter 2

The Retelling of Mughal-e-Azam:
The Birth and Death of Anarkali
by Professor Soumyabrat Choudhry

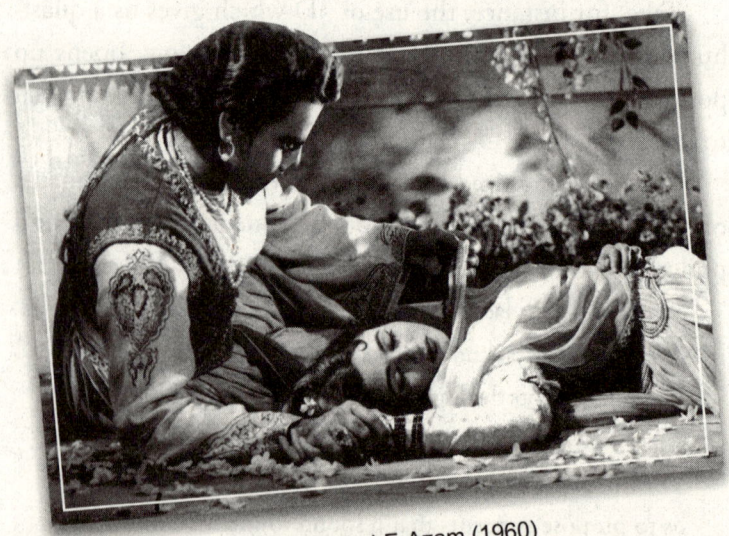

Fig.2 Mughal-E-Azam (1960)

PROFESSOR Soumyabrat Choudhry of the School of Arts and Aesthetics at JNU decodes the mystique of Madhubala–the actress herself and the character of Anarkali that she portrays in the 1960 film, Mughal-e-Azam. The professor assiduously peels off layer after layer of meaning behind the unforgettable sequences and dialogues, tracing an intricate, and hitherto unseen pattern in a film that has left such an indelible mark on its viewers, both in India and amongst the Indian Diaspora abroad. The following is a transcription of a lecture delivered at the Symposium at Janki Devi Memorial College.

Let us set the scene first.

The *sangtarash* (sculptor) is assigned the task of making something beautiful and extraordinary for the grand occasion of the adored, combat-weary son of Emperor Akbar, returning home from his exploits on the battlefield. The father's heart is bursting with pride and the mother's with love as they wait to embrace him. The sculptor understands the enormity of his task and sets out to create the most beautiful statue of a woman; one to be unveiled when the Prince arrives at the celebrations. Only he is not able to finish it in time and the day of unveiling is already upon him. What can he do? He has a clever idea–Nadira, a common working woman's equally common daughter, an extraordinarily beautiful nobody, is requested to substitute as the statue for the night of the function. He drills it into her that she must stand in a very still and graceful pose, to imitate a statue wrought in alabaster!

Thence begins the story of the ill-fated romance between Salim, the redoubtable son of the arrogant Emperor Akbar, and the commoner Nadira, whose uncommon beauty urges the emperor to bestow upon her the exotic moniker, Anarkali–Pomegranate Blossom!!

Professor Soumyabrat trains his keen eyes on this epic historical drama, unfolding its many layers of meaning and exposing the social mores, the deviousness of human character, the arrogance of ruthless emperors, and the rebelliousness of the human spirit that will not succumb to the vicissitudes of fate–all of which the filmmaker K. Asif weaves into the plot of a film that is unsurpassed to this day for its dramatic power. As he proceeds, Professor Soumyabrat allows his theoretical insights to be coloured by his awe of the actress Madhubala's beauty, his pity for a woman scorned by the man she loves in real life, that is, her co-star Dilip Kumar, and her vulnerability before a body that is being progressively destroyed by disease even while she is powerless to save herself.

His analysis begins with the sculptor's execution of his gargantuan task, given the fact that he has promised to create a statue of such unsurpassed beauty that, when beheld, will compel an Emperor to take off his crown, a soldier to take out his sword, and a common man his heart, just to make oblation at the feet of its possessor.

He creates the most beautiful thing on earth–but being a 'thing', it must be fixed in its passivity. This passivity is stamped as it were on Anarkali/Madhubala's character from day one. She is objectified and must identify with the object with which, as she is told by the *sangtarash*, the prince has fallen in love at first sight.

It is Salim's reaction and initiation into love that makes for a more interesting study. Love blossoms in the young prince's heart as soon as he beholds her (the statue's) incredible beauty in secret. The audience however realises that the love affair is doomed from the beginning. The State soothsayer has prophesied that it would be ill-omened for the prince to look upon any idol before daybreak but the prince, impatient to see for himself what the sculptor's claims could amount to, invites his doom by stealing into the hall in the dead of night to take a peek at the idol, in defiance of the soothsayer's warning.

Love stirs in his heart and is almost instantaneously elevated to the status of worship! He is awestruck by the beauty of what he believes to be a statue, and he confesses to his friend the urge to acknowledge the presence of the divine in an idol. He would be accused of idolatry (which is sinful in Islam), his friend admonishes, to which again his quick rejoinder is to stubbornly claim that he would at least be lauded for his faithfulness to the object of his love!

The dialogues are in Urdu, penned by Amanullah Khan, in collaboration with Wajahat Mirza, Kamaal Amrohi, and Ehsan Rizvi, having the power to evoke visions and capture emotions and situations like no other language could have! Take for instance the words used for idolatry, *but parasti*, and faithfulness, *wafa parasti*, which convey complex ideas that cannot admit to any straightforward rendition.

Soumyabrat calls our attention to the interesting fact that Salim falls in love with the statue of Madhubala even before he watches her transform into a living woman. He falls in love with a piece of stone! Thus, the real woman is objectified in two ways—in terms of her worth as the most beautiful statue, an object, which implies a market worth, but she is also objectified by the lover's gaze that freezes her worth in stone, as the 'most beautiful thing'. In Sartre's vocabulary, she gets objectified and transfixed in the look of the other!

In this process of being objectified, the woman presents herself as absolute passivity. One does not know what she feels or thinks! Indeed, she does not know herself. She has yet to acquire her identity as Anarkali, which will define her to herself, though falsely, as we find out when the story progresses. It is at the cusp of the two opposites of human frailty—the complete sexual passivity of being represented through stone and the all too human passion of first love that floods the soul—in her case tempered by the fear of being unworthy of a prince's love and fidelity, that Madhubala, the actress, is born! She portrays Anarkali with aplomb, exploring her own potential to emote through every expression, every limb. It is clear that she is playing herself here, as the lines between acting a part and living an experience begin to blur.

At first, Anarkali finds herself thrust into the scene of love without yet actively participating in it. But love is quickly ignited when Salim writes her a note expressing his agitation, and when she looks into his smouldering eyes under the constant prodding of her teasing, coquettish little sister. The film's central theme is romantic love and its appeal rests almost entirely on how that love and romance plays out between the two lead actors, the manly and impossibly attractive Dilip Kumar, and the frail and feminine, the indomitable and matchless, Madhubala!

As love takes wings and soars, its soft whisperings float and waft through the corridors of the palace until–aided by the machinations of the wicked vamp–they reach the ears of the emperor. Now this scene of love quickly transforms into a scene of politics as the prince's desire for her must negotiate with the father's obdurate intention to deny him this bounty, all for his obstinate stand that a ruler cannot bow to the aspirations of lowly commoners.

Before learning of her love for the prince, the emperor expresses unstinting pleasure at the girl's bold subterfuge, standing in place of the statue, and fearlessly continuing to hold her pose even while the prince shoots an arrow at her to unveil what he believes to be a sculpture in stone. The emperor orders her to present a dance in court on the occasion of *Navroz* (Iranian or Persian New Year and the first day of Spring); a dance which he watches with great relish! It is, after all, the usual practice in any feudal society, to make young nubile slave girls dance and perform in the courts of kings and noblemen.

His attitude towards Anarkali begins to change as he learns about his son's indiscretions. Akbar dreams big for his son and he is beside himself with anger at the thought that Salim would squander everything away by dallying with a servant girl. His emotions, masterfully portrayed by Prithviraj Kapoor in a role of a lifetime, range from indulgence to annoyance to anger and then to hatred, which he spews out from time to time through venomous epithets. Now he addresses her derisively as '*tu*' (a loosely used address used instead of 'you'), marking her out as one who deserves no courtesy. He calls her alternatively, a *kaneez* (servant girl), a *bandi* (slave girl), an *aandhi* (storm), a *fitnah* (temptress), a *naagin* (serpent), a *laundi* (a handmaid), and a *rakkasa* (whore), his voice spilling utter contempt and degradation!

Durjan, Salim's friend and confidante, cautions the latter to be patient. He explains that a father's soaring ambitions of consolidating and expanding his empire through grand and profitable marriage alliances of his son with the daughters of neighbouring kings and noblemen have come crashing down. All due to the discovery of his son's servile prostrations before a servant girl.

Time and again Akbar demonstrates his authority and displays his complete sexual sovereignty—when he indulgently bestows upon her the title of Anarkali or when he commands her to perform at the *Navroz* festival. This is also evident when he sets her free with the injunction that she must give Salim the impression that she prefers Akbar's rewards of riches to Salim's feelings for her! In that sense, this is a clash between a father and son for sexual dominance! Prithviraj Kapoor's stately physique and his voice are riveting. They fit the image of a ruthless emperor like a glove. His acting is superb as well.

But it is Madhubala's prowess as an actor that Soumyabrat focuses on. The manner in which she uses her dance and her stylized gestures—those very things that make the king treat her with such contempt–to challenge the emperor's might, is vintage Madhubala! Professor Soumyabrat analyses one of the most dramatically intense scenes in the movie, Madhubala's dance of defiance, through which she teaches the mighty emperor one of the greatest lessons of his life–humility! It is a scene that the director, the lyricist, and the producer realised would be the highest point of this tragic story that takes on the proportions of a Greek Tragedy! Thus, the otherwise black and white film turns into colour from here on! The opulence and grandeur of the settings and the dramatic impact of the onscreen action could never have been conveyed had the filmmakers persisted with black and white.

Akbar's initial expectations are that he will be treated to a delightful performance and at the same time have the satisfaction of removing the servant girl from his son's life forever. These are not ill-founded expectations as he has commanded her to do so and who would dare disobey the emperor's bidding?

But as the song begins to play Akbar realises that the slave girl is literally singing a different tune. Shakeel Badayuni's lyrics, Naushad's composition, Lata Mangeshkar's voice, and Madhubala's performance, all come together to create magic on screen! The song and the dance are an amalgamation of religious supplication, vanity, defiance, raw courage, an unabashed avowal of love, and a speaking of truth to power– all executed to perfection by Madhubala.

No less is the portrayal of Akbar. It is reported that Prithviraj Kapoor had to use smoke or some sort of smoke-causing material so that his eyes would sting and take on a bloodshot look. In the film, his wrath bellows forth through those bloodshot eyes as he hits the armrests of his throne with palpable force.

With her expression changing swiftly from soft devotion towards God to scorn for the ruler she sings the beautiful lines in Urdu,

Purdah nahin jab koi khuda se, bandon se purdah karna kya.

When there is no purdah (veiling) before the Almighty himself what need is there for purdah before a servant of the Almighty?

The lines from the song walk away with all the applause; it is sheer poetry!

The word *banda* is also a synonym for slave! Thus, Anarkali manages with her words, not only to shame the arrogant Akbar into lowering his eyes but also to bring him down to her level as an equal for they are both servants of God; they are both slaves! In this epic moment, she proclaims her triumph over the mightiest of the mighty!

Of course, Akbar cannot allow his insult at the hands of a slave girl to go unpunished. He tries to hide his mortification behind taunts and ridicule as he orders his men to throw her into the dark dungeons of the prison. Only this time, his words do not evoke fear. Anarkali brushes away the restraining hands of the prison guard and with her head held high, she turns to make an exaggerated gesture of obeisance that punctures the emperor's vanity utterly.

Madhubala as Anarkali is now in prison, bound in chains

too heavy for her slight frame! In reality, the actress had a perforated heart from birth and was already very ill during the filming of *Mughal-e-Azam*. She suffered from a broken heart in more ways than one. Her love affair with her co-star Dilip Kumar had crashed and he had already turned away from his promises of marriage. It is reported that Madhubala, whose real name was Begum Mumtaz Jahan Dehalvi, and Dilip Kumar were not even on speaking terms when the shooting for the film was at its height. She died of heart failure not long after, at the tender age of thirty-six.

The actress was conscious of her ethereal face, which had set the standard of beauty in Bollywood. Professor Soumyabrat compares her to the exquisite Katya Orlova (Michelle Pfeiffer), a Russian woman about whom Barley Blair (Sean Connery), the protagonist of the film, *The Russia House*, (adapted from John Le Carre's novel of the same name) says, 'With a face like that who needs a body?'

But the ravages of illness were starting to show, and Madhubala and the director K. Asif had to take great pains to camouflage the signs. After all, she was a star and she was playing the role of a lifetime. She had to be presented as Anarkali, the most beautiful woman. Madhubala hid her wan looks and pallor behind makeup that transformed her into looking her radiant best; a fact that no doubt contributed to the film's lasting aura.

Anarkali is imprisoned and at Akbar's mercy. She must be ground under his heels for being insolent and daring to challenge his power. Moreover, she has committed the unpardonable sin of alienating him from his only beloved son. Akbar is certain that the darkness within the prison walls and being strapped in chains like an animal would destroy her spirit and he would get his sweet revenge. Madhubala is without her makeup now! It is a symbolic stripping away of her makeup to show how beauty and womanhood must be reduced to dust. She now stands before the emperor, bareheaded and sans makeup, small and vulnerable, as Akbar pronounces his final indictment!

It is believed that these scenes not only stripped her of makeup, they also stripped her of the last vestiges of hope and strength in real life. Her skin was badly lacerated from the heavy chains which she had to lift high in a couple of scenes. The well-known radio announcer, Amin Sayani, revealed on his show with Filmfare that he had interviewed many of her relatives only to learn how Madhubala never recovered from her exertions during those scenes on the sets of *Mughal-e-Azam*.

Anarkali is sentenced to death and Raja Maan Singh graciously asks her if she has any last wishes. Her words mumbled with trembling lips leave the emperor and his trusted companion astounded! She tells them that she would like to become the queen of Hindustan before she dies! Filled with derision Akbar mocks her for not giving up her true aspirations even in the face of impending death! But Anarkali explains how her only desire is to uphold Salim's commitment to her. Salim had vowed that he would one day make her the queen and she had to prevent him from having to labour under lifelong shame and guilt for having failed to keep his words to a mere servant girl.

The king scripts a ghastly punishment for Anarkali who

is finally at his mercy—she is to be cemented alive inside a tomb of bricks and mortar. But before that, she must also do the emperor a favour. She must drug the prince into a stupor so that his men can snatch her from her lover's embrace, leaving him to believe for the rest of his life that he has been betrayed. It is a punishment of epic proportions like the kind one finds in Greek tragedies. Antigone, the daughter of Oedipus, for instance, was indicted by Creon, the King of Thebes, and awarded a similar punishment of being buried alive for her disobedience. As she prepares to meet her fate in the film, Madhubala the actress morphs into Anarkali the maid, smitten by an impossible and doomed love for a prince.

The wicked, scheming Bahaar, who has had her daggers in Anarkali from the very beginning, sings to the two newlyweds and her words are both in praise of love but also a warning about what is to come afterwards. Anarkali's beauty comes to splendorous life as she sits on her nuptial couch with her husband for one night. It is not clear in the film whether the nuptials have been read and Salim and Anarkali are truly husband and wife for one night, but at least Salim believes so. He is beside himself with the impatience to own her body and soul. The sensuousness of the scene where only a feather comes between the passionate lips of the prince and his bride, was a talking point of the film, especially as the two actors at the time barely acknowledged each other's presence in real life.

As the prince falls into a faint at the feet of his beloved, all animation leaves her face and she is escorted out of her marriage chamber, dead from within and without. The beauty that was not her fault but for which she has to pay with her life is extinguished forever.

This sequence marks an end in many ways—the dramatic end of the film, the end of the ill-fated love between Salim and Anarkali, the end (death) of Anarkali, the end of Madhubala's own love affair with Dilip Kumar, and the beginning of the end of the actress herself.

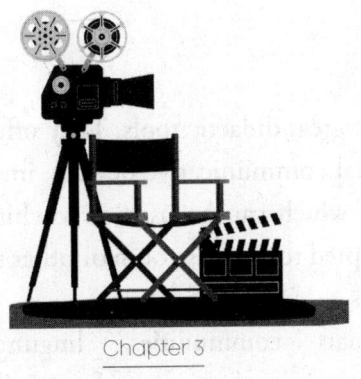

Chapter 3

Film and Culture:
Inviting New Voices and Newer Visions

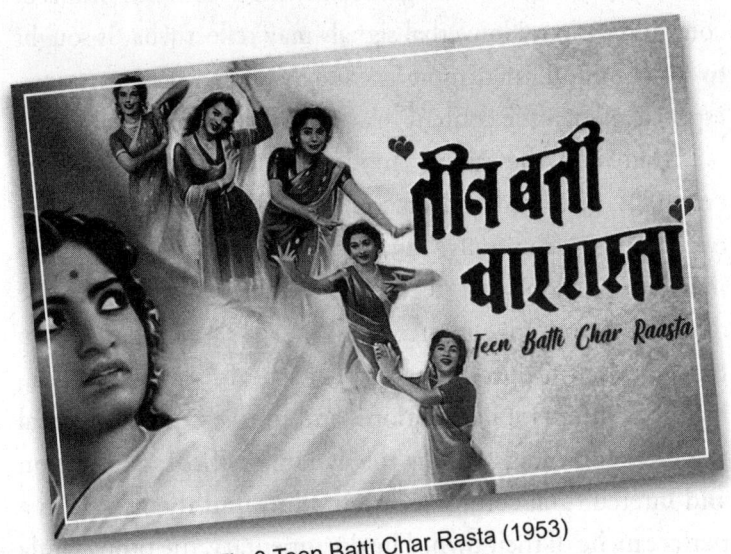

Fig.3 Teen Batti Char Rasta (1953)

FILMS make great didactic tools. They offer an entire range of audio-visual communicative devices, images, speech, and music, all of which can be used as teaching strategies that are easily adapted to the classroom or other teaching-learning environments.

In human communities, linguistic modes of communication are always supplemented by non-verbal modes. Some of these are basic and include body language, posture, facial expressions, tone and inflection of voice, sound, silence, etc. Mime, songlike story narratives, metaphors crafted in art, and even food, are significantly more complex means of communication. Nonverbal signals may reflect what is sought to be communicated more accurately than verbal messages, especially when the content relates to sociocultural realities.

Many of the above modes of communication are culturally mediated and successful communication depends on correct, culturally nuanced, interpretation. In an increasingly globalised, technologically advanced world, the demand for effective intercultural means of communication has increased in just about any field–healthcare, education, business, international relations, and tourism. As intellectual resources for understanding the dynamics of communication and intercultural communication, films find themselves in a perfect niche of their own. The documentary, the propaganda film, and the historical or period film are popular modes of communication and the measurement of their success lies in how the film is received by an audience, both at home and away. There is a burgeoning interest across schools and colleges to include the use of cinema within formal subjects of study such as Communication Theory, Intercultural Communications, and Information Theory.

Even while films tend to sometimes exaggerate or downplay cultural meaning or distort cultural representations to achieve an intended dramatic effect, they nevertheless prove to be extremely effective in helping students decipher foreign cultures and understand the nuances of cultural theories and concepts. Lustig and Koester have defined Intercultural Communication as, 'a symbolic, interpretive, transactional, contextual process, in which people from different cultures create shared meanings'.[1] Films reveal these shared meanings as they range over an entire gamut of issues common to people from any corner of the world, cutting across cultures and geographical boundaries. Human emotions such as love, compassion, fear or hatred; experiences of coming of age, anxiety, and loneliness; the building or loss of trust; racial, ethnic, or sexual identity; inequities of wealth, gender, power, and privilege—integrating film clips into classroom teaching is a forceful way of illustrating these commonalities.

The relationship of films with the content they exhibit is a symbiotic one. Events in its history, its social, cultural, and political practices, and its crisis, all have an impact on the nation's cinematic expression, and these expressions, in turn, provide a window into its cultural and social history. Cinema stimulates curiosity. It develops a predisposition in students to think critically and analytically about the realities of life lived differently, about cross-cultural interactions between people from different cultures, and about the different manners of overcoming a possible culture clash and forging healthier interpersonal relations. This promotes tolerance and inclusivity among people, enhances their emotional and psychological growth, and leads to an overall sense of well-being.

We traced a myriad of scholarly insights in this area, coming from the symposium presentations of speakers from the field. These voices shed light on the important subject of films as a means of communicating culture, sparking great interest in the young student researchers present at the event.

Vebhuti Duggal: Community Listening Practices and Film Music

Dr Vebhuti Duggal, a teacher at Ambedkar University Delhi, described as part of the social imaginary of the times, particularly during the first two decades of post-independence India, the unique listening practices exemplified by *farmaishi* radio programs—the practice of people writing requests to radio stations to play songs from popular Hindi films.[2] Her account included descriptive portrayals of the listeners, the radio personalities, and fan magazines of this period.

Vebhuti's arguments are primarily based on how the *farmaish* (song request) related practices of listening, constituted a unique mediated form of listening that enriched the experience of film music when enjoyed by a community of listeners. Using the song request radio program as a sonic map, she examines the unifying properties of such community listening practices in which a film song becomes a metonym for a particular type of film experience away from the physical space and time circumscribed by the cinema hall. Not only do such practices represent an immeasurable aspect of audience reception of cinema, but they also point to the potential of popular cinema to forge connections among individuals who are total strangers to one another. They provide an ideal setting in which people, by their common interests, habits, and longings, are drawn uniquely together under local surroundings and bound by unusual acts of recognition.

Mahiema Anand: Filmmaker, Explorer, and Seeker

Mahiema Anand, an Indian filmmaker and storyteller who describes herself as an explorer and seeker, recounts the many enriching experiences she has had, journeying through this 'world of wonders' as she describes it. For her, it was like living one full life, and she translated these experiences into her films with great honesty in order to entertain as well as enhance collective knowledge. At the symposium, Mahiema spoke of her responsibility not just towards her audience and her artistic self, but also her responsibility towards cinema as the creative art that became the chosen vehicle to convey her insights and her experiences.

How does art act as a catalyst for change? The process begins from the moment of choosing a creative path from several options—writing, sculpting, painting, filmmaking, or dance. One needs to be extra careful while choosing a path of exploration and be aware of the reasons behind that choice, says Mahiema, as this will define the future trajectory of a creative product.

She believes that to create something meaningful it is crucial to de-condition oneself from how one is brought up, even though the process of de-conditioning is fraught with difficulty. We are products of our surroundings and de-conditioning makes the journey ahead a difficult one. She had her phase of de-conditioning while living abroad and exploring opportunities there. She says, 'When I landed there, I didn't know what to do, I had no money so I painted houses, I worked in bars, I washed dishes, and did whatever you may say (sic)…'

During the course of it, she came across a documentary filmmaker with whose help she became acquainted with the craft enough to delve into unexplored areas of filmmaking and creativity. In her own words,

> He had put that seed in my mind, you know that passion; and as Sudipto has said, it was the passion which he had seen in his own sister's eyes. I saw it in his (her new acquaintance's) eyes…and it was like I knew there was nothing else that I could do in my life from then on.[3]

Each of Mahiema's films tells a fascinating story. On returning to India, her first assignment was for BBC Wales. She began work in 1988, on a series based on the lives of prominent women in India. It proved to be a turning point in her career. As she developed a deeper understanding of cinema and began analysing it from fresh perspectives, her confidence grew. She made several documentaries and docudramas that mirrored her own experiences, reflecting different aspects of human life. As she journeyed forth with her equipment and team into a familiar world inhabited by the common masses, her creative urges prompted her to transcend the boundaries of self-centrism and cast aside the surface trivialities of mundane life.

Once, while working on a project on Down syndrome in Singapore, Mahiema decided to portray the theme of the film in all its rawness, shorn of all aesthetic adornment, believing that she would thus be able to infuse sincerity and authenticity into it. She was eager to enhance its impact and stay closely engaged with its future course. Such projects, according to her, were emotionally challenging but left a deep mark both on the filmmaker and the viewer, sensitising them towards the sorrows of others while making them reflect on what they could offer to the community. She wanted her films to encourage viewers to ask themselves, 'What is it that I can do to make people's lives better, however short it is'. For her film on Down syndrome, she did intensive research about patients who were thus afflicted and was amazed to find that they had an extra chromosome that made them different–extra compassionate, loving, creative, talented, and exuberant. She made it a central point of her film to tell the world that people with this affliction were special and unique.

Film on Aghoris: Addressing Much-Awaited Change

Mahiema Anand had an interesting story to tell with her film on the life of Aghoris, commissioned by Columbia Tristar. By her admission, this film helped her grow as a docudrama maker and sharpened her filmmaking abilities. Aghoris have been a much-feared sect, owing to the common belief that they ate the flesh of the dead. Many discouraged her and advised her not to work on the subject as the Aghoris were reputed to be vile and dangerous, having strange *tantric* powers. Undeterred by all such warnings, she landed one fine day in Varanasi and proceeded to get in touch with this sect of *Sadhus*. Her foreign collaborators would refer to them as 'cannibals', which displeased her excessively. She could not fathom why a community that followed the dictates of their cult and was faithful to their practices, should be so defamed.

She studied the Aghoris closely, and they, for their part, allowed her to come up close and observe their daily lifestyle and their quaint rituals. India is often known as a land of snake charmers in countries abroad. Mahiema attempted to redefine and re-create the idea of an India free of such exotic misconceptions. She instructed the members of her unit to absorb the energy and get a feel of the place and the people. They had to decide on a crucial detail,

> ...what is it that we can offer in the film? I didn't want to make a sensational film because it's very easy to make a sensational film out of the subject that I was offered... because what they do is sensational. But I said no, it is also very important to be able to bring out the truth behind what they do. I didn't realise then that this was also going to be a huge landmark event for me as a filmmaker.

An equally important project was a film based on people with leprosy called *Colours of Life: Curing Leprosy with*

Compassion at Shanti Sewa Griha. There was a time when leprosy was considered a highly contagious disease and those afflicted with it were shunned and banished from human habitations as outcasts. The film is about a beautiful and willful German woman who had a life-changing experience because of a tour guide she met during an excursion to Nepal. When the guide asked her if she would be willing to adopt a child born to parents who were both suffering from leprosy, her response was in the affirmative. This life-transforming decision gave Marianne Grosspietsch, the lady in question, the resolve to establish the first Shanti Leprahilfe aid organisation for lepers in 1992. She was determined to extend a helping hand to many such people, and it has remained a part of her journey for the past twenty-six years. The child she adopted is now a grown-up boy currently living a happy life in Germany as a result of her courageous choice. The film directed by Mahiema Anand is about Marianna's Centre, *Shanti Sewa Griha* in Kathmandu, Nepal, established in collaboration with Shanti Leprahilfe Dortmund e.V. (Germany) and registered with the Social Welfare Council of Nepal. The story of Marianne Grosspietsch's Shanti Sewa Griha is truly inspirational, and Mahiema's film remains a witness to her success.

Vani Subramanian: Gender and the Cinematic Space

Vani Subramanian, a documentary filmmaker, takes a critical look at how gender is defined in the cinematic space. Though safety is a central concern in whichever space women find themselves, Vani takes a broader perspective not confined to the questions of safety alone, which she thinks is but one aspect of our lives. She looks at the myriad other things that shape the lives of women; all sorts of occupations, belongings, existential experiences of being and becoming, having the good fortune of living the life of a grown woman or of not being allowed to grow out of the shadows at all, and much else that form the textured qualities of our lived spaces. For Vani, these explorations promised to be fulfilling ones, and they go on to become the primary focus of a lifelong enterprise.

When Vani Subramanian does workshops on cities and spaces, she takes a flexible approach, quoting women often and paying heed to all manner of experiences that shape a woman's life. Part of her work has been to look at popular films and examine the role of space in cinema, in the context of the construction of gender.

She looks at cinematic spaces as constituted by complex codes that operate between the viewer and the filmmaker. The film tells you something about the characters, moments, plots, and moral values of the times, but there is always more happening, literally, behind the scenes. As a documentary filmmaker, she frames her subject with a deep eye, tracking how the characters may be projected, where the film is located, and what the moving images convey.

Often in films, you find a moment when the protagonist or a character actor says '*Mai kahan hoon?*' Where am I? Implicitly, there is that other question, 'Who am I?' or '*Main kaun hoon?*' The meaning of these questions would be constituted by different factors such as locations or sets; even the mental condition of the character. Such factors are particular to a film grounding its characters. But characters can be representative; in different roles, in different films, at different locations, and especially in different cinematic spaces, a character will mean vastly different things when she asks 'Where am I?' In a documentary film, such a question is taken literally and the answer must have a specific reference. As a documentary filmmaker, Vani finds it a major challenge to map a strange location, being constrained by the unknown realities of that location.

As an aside, Vani Subramanian compares Indian television serials to Pakistani TV dramas and points to the contrasting spaces and sets created in the two separate contexts. She cites this as a major factor accounting for the former being less credible than the latter. The reality that a serialised show or pulp film in India depicts is wholly subjective depending on the views and preferences of the filmmaker. Popular cinema or television is escapist, its primary aim being to keep the audience entertained. There is no compulsion to adhere to any norms of veracity or aesthetics. The plots revolve around an assortment of moral and social values in alignment with the beliefs and perceptions of the spectators, and the filmmaker connects with the audience via the same. Architecture, location, and film sets are all integral parts of the film, helping the maker flesh out the dimensions of the characters and plot. From popular cinema to documentary films, these elements form the repertoire from which the film is crafted. But while popular cinema can get away with taking enormous liberties with any or all of these without compromising the worth of the film, a documentary cannot.

The Nation, Family, or Home are clearly defined spaces in popular Indian cinema. The idea of the Nation as territory is often what anchors the plot and characters of a film. Such was the archetypal 1953 film *Teen Batti Char Rasta*, directed by a progressive-minded V. Shantaram, which offered the family as a metaphorical space for the Nation. The film is about six protagonists from different provinces, five out of whom are married to women with different ethnic roots. '*Teen Batti Char Rasta*' is a euphemism for the home address of the family patriarch who wants an ideal 'home' for his sons and their brides (the crossroads where their home is situated bears the name 'Teen Batti'). The three lights stand for love, learning, and loyalty, and the crossroads formed by the four roads provide a meeting point for the women coming from four corners of the country. The female lead who finally marries the sixth son is dusky and plain-looking, and therefore spurned by the boy until he comes to his senses when he sees the 'beautiful' person within. The intent of the director to address gender emancipation, in however understated a fashion, is evident. The film was a straightforward metaphor for national unity and cultural integration.

Teen Batti Char Rasta also paved the way for Indian cinema's subsequent use of the great Indian joint family as a space in which to convey everything, from human relations to wildly swinging individual fortunes, to jealousy, love, loneliness, alienation, and forbidden emotions.

Popular Indian cinema also uses the 'home' as a space that shapes its characters and plot. The home is where everyone must return to in the end. It is to the home that the prodigal son, the errant 'hero' (never a daughter), returns. The 'hero' is the principal protagonist, whatever his background credentials might be; whether from a poor family or a Robinhood-style hero. Whether a Casanova or the Romeo sort, a working man, farmer, dacoit, or nationalist, all such figures resonate with the sensibilities of the common man–speaking of the 50s and 60s. The home is also the 'space' where the woman realises her true calling and finds her safety and protection.

While a justification for the presence of the male lead in a film is not required, for he is simply 'what the film is about', a clear rationalisation is offered for a female character being in the film. She is most often there for a romantic interlude with the 'hero'. Female characters are circumscribed by the male gaze. There is a rigid moral framework of values that women must adhere to, which dictates what is honourable conduct for them. The female lead in a film is typically equated with virtues that are prescribed by the unambiguously patriarchal structures that surround her; something that does not limit the actions of the male lead.

Other roles assigned to women are of a sister or sister-in-law, a vamp, or the mother of the 'hero'. The mother embodies the moral compass of the entire family. Even when she is shown to be domineering, her presence is strongly bound to the home and becomes identical to it. Irrespective of what her role is, a film shows the home as the space designated for a woman. And the home becomes the metaphor for virtue, for blissful domesticity, and for living happily ever after.

In many films, for instance in Mani Ratnam's *Roja* or Yash Chopra's *Dil Toh Pagal Hai*, the 'heroine' begins by being shown as a 'free spirit', naïve and docile maybe, but all the same, she is her own person. However, as the film progresses towards its climax, she is shown undergoing certain experiences that show her the virtues of conforming to tradition and custom, for she can never be shown breaking the glass ceiling of patriarchy.

A Shabana Azmi may be shown as a defiant pickpocket at the beginning of the film, in this case, a Manmohan Desai masala blockbuster, *Amar Akbar Anthony* (1972); a common thief who gets arrested by the 'hero'. But by the time the film reaches its end, she has been reformed as a result of the love she receives from the same police inspector who arrested her in the first place, and who holds out the promise of a respectable life after she marries him. Kajol in *Kuch Kuch Hota Hai* (Karan Johar, 1998) must transform from a gawky, jeans-clad tomboy, to a demure Indian beauty in a traditional saree, to win the 'hero'. It is the deep-rooted patriarchal predilections of the predominantly male moviemaker's fraternity that force female actors towards such stereotypical film roles.

Anandana Kapur: The Interactivity, Immersion, and Impact of Cinema Today

Anandana Kapur, a filmmaker and media scholar based out of New Delhi, is interested in telling unique Indian stories through her films. Viewers' relationship with cinema, their experience of a story unfolding on screen, has changed dynamically she says. People are getting more and more accustomed to watching movies from within the comfort of their homes, on television screens, personal theatres, or any other screening devices. The interactive bend in cinematic trends has gone beyond reels or projectors to include commonly used tools such as mobile phones and tablets, even though access to e-resources remains a distant dream for many in India.

The three terms, namely interactivity, immersion, and impact, help her to analyse the changing realities of the times. To her, cinema is all about stories and unfortunately, we are looking at a time when unique stories are fast drying up. We live in a hypertext economy in which everything is connected with everything else through a convergence of technology, entertainment, knowledge, and politics. Today, it is easy to make movies with a global look and feel but the storylines are missing. The story as a format has to be reinvented in this new context of space and time and the expanding horizons of knowledge. Every so often a film is left open-ended, preventing foreclosure to a story. At other times, a filmmaker looking for different ways of storytelling joins through mental imaging or synchronisation, a story encrypted within the film to bits of relevant information outside of it or to fragments of other stories, leaving open the possibility of a sequel or sequels. In the hypertext architecture, we are performing knowledge. But there is also a clear need for a more critical and ethical engagement with the virtual world, for which a good story is an excellent medium.

Everything about films has become mechanical. Currently, there is a lot of auto-ethnographic work being produced. In academic social science research, for instance, students make ethnographic films as part fulfilment of a project requirement, by documenting cultures and their practices with methodical precision and technical competence. Ethnographic films conform to a different set of criteria than documentary films. They can be made with handheld cameras and mobile phones, giving them that extra touch of reality. Professional filmmakers have had to acknowledge the work of ethnographic filmmakers and are often tempted to improvise on their techniques to align their work and vocabulary with the latter's style of filmmaking.

In an era in which the use of Artificial intelligence (AI) to create art is being increasingly explored, one may question the forced homogenisation of art, overlooking the fact that it is specific to individual artists who differ from one another in sensibility, style, perspective, and comprehension of things. Should filmmakers challenge the use of artificial intelligence or harness it for the betterment of cinema? That has become a moot question.

The auteur notion of filmmaking has also lost much of its sheen along the way. The days of a filmmaker, the artist and author of the film, being considered of paramount importance to the exclusion of other aspects such as its subject or genre, are fast disappearing. Not so long ago, the director who oversaw all audio and visual elements, and exercised a highly centralised and subjective control on most aspects of the film could own 'authorship', pushing to the sidelines the writer of the screenplay, the cinematographer, and everyone else involved in the creative process. That has now changed. With cinema becoming overwhelmingly audience-oriented, there are new imperatives for filmmakers. 'How to reach a target audience? How do we discover the invisible voices wanting to be heard? How do we make films available and easily accessible from various devices and locations? What form of circulation and what platform for screening would be best for a film–a popular broadcasting channel, video links, cable television, or OTT platforms?' These are the central questions that occupy the filmmakers of today and the answers emerge through collaborative effort. The ultimate worth and recall value of a film is a collective goal, says Anandana.

India in a Day, one of India's largest crowdsourced films of recent times, is a good example. It is a feature-length documentary on the life of common people in the country, made in 2016 by director Richie Mehta. The film was made by working painstakingly on the footage curated from more than 16,000 videos about unheard real-life stories that were submitted in a single day by members of the public from across India. The contributors as well as the lead characters in the movie being the common people, the film claimed to represent art 'of and for' the public, created through people's labour, challenging the usual institutionalised manner of film architecture.

Anandana's film, *Aashiyan*, is another such example. It is an interactive documentary about homemakers and domestic workers hailing from the less affluent parts of Delhi. A montage of women-centric stories from the metropolis, filmed on a mobile phone because of its deep reach and accessibility, *Aashiyan*, which in Hindi means a haven, was the name chosen by the women themselves. *Aashiyan* is also the name of the interactive mobile app that gives domestic workers a platform to represent themselves through everyday conversations about the safety concerns of women, and the dehumanising impact of the backbreaking daily struggles of city life. Accompanied by an audio-visual gallery, the app allows the listener to understand and be part of the ongoing conversation about the aspirations, disappointments, and accomplishments of the 'daily help'.[4]

Filmmakers must navigate through multiple layers of social life to create meaning out of the flux. Films mirror who we are as individuals, both in personal and public life, and this 'mirroring' comes in the way of conveying things the way they are. Even though at one level filmmaking is a deeply self-reflective exercise that involves projecting the world through one's own eyes, a filmmaker must consciously set aside the self-actualising, individualistic aspects of filmmaking, and concentrate on the political instead, always keeping an objective eye. They must avoid getting lost amidst personal adversities and struggles. The constant tussle between what one wishes to project, or thinks ought to be projected, versus projecting reality as it is, is mediated by the strong need to present the missed-out subtleties of human connectedness. The appetite for innovative depictions of life tears through idleness, pullbacks, and prejudices. While what one sees on the screen looks impeccable, a lot of intellectual labour, the overcoming of personal struggles, and the suppression of one's unfulfilled expectations go into its making. A lot of progress has been made in the direction of pathbreaking innovations in filmmaking and a lot more is coming up by the day, promising a complete overhaul of the old modalities in times to come.

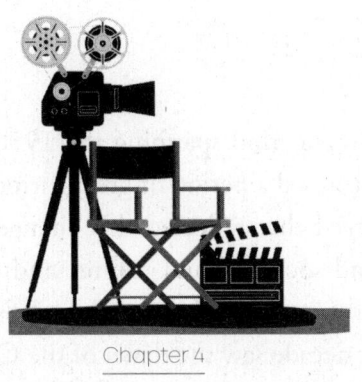

Chapter 4

The Resurgence of Film:
The Arrival of Parallel Cinema and the New Wave

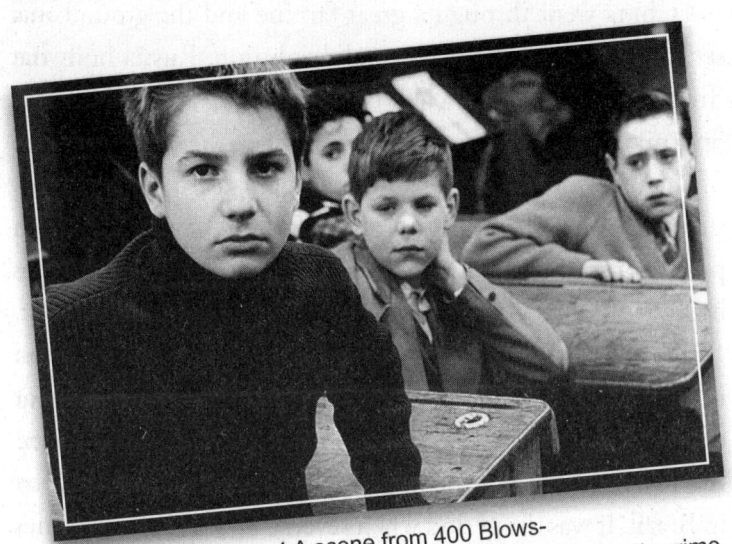

Fig.4 A scene from 400 Blows- A young boy, left without attention, strays into a life of petty crime.

IN the post-war period spanning the 1950s and 60s, when the world witnessed a period of great turmoil, a new kind of cinema emerged that reflected this change in the political, economic, and socio-cultural realms, and even contributed to it in important ways. In the United States of America, this post-war decade saw the dawn of the Cold War with the Soviet Union, the dirty war with Vietnam, the launching of the Civil Rights movement, the 'baby boom', the beginning of the so-called 'glorious age' of American capitalism and the detonation of the first hydrogen bomb.

China went through a great famine and the ground was set for Chairman Mao's cultural revolution. Russia built the 'Iron Curtain' and launched the first artificial earth satellite, Sputnik. The Western hemisphere saw the establishment of the first communist regime by Fidel Castro in Cuba and the formation of the European Economic Community, the precursor to the EU. Everest was conquered for the first time by Tenzin Norgay and Edmund Hillary.

The period was also marked by the shocking assassinations of Martin Luther King Jr. and Robert Kennedy, the launching of NASA and NATO, India's adoption of its Constitution, the Korean War, and the beginning of the FIFA World Cup in Brazil. It was the period when several 'new waves' in cinema took shape in different countries, attempting to capture the tumultuous transformations the world was going through.

The French 'Nouvelle Vague', or New Wave was the best known amongst these, giving its name to all other similar national cinema movements, also referred to as 'new cinema' or 'young cinema', across the world.

French New Wave

The French New Wave is considered to be one of the most significant cinema movements anywhere in the world—one that revolutionised the art of filmmaking forever. It began around the late 1940s with a group of French critics who wrote for the influential film journal *Cahiers du Cinema* and who were critical of mainstream cinema, which to their mind had lost all touch with this fast-changing world and the lives of people caught in the flux. They found that the conservative style and aesthetics characterising classic French, British, German, and American films failed to enhance their ability to capture true human emotion or to provide an understanding of the human condition. They were especially dismissive of the French industry's big-budget commercial films, the so-called 'tradition of quality' films that were well-structured pieces curated out of literary masterpieces, with neatly rounded plots, elaborate dialogues, impeccable camerawork, and accomplished actors. Finding these films completely lacking in authenticity and sincerity, the *Cahiers* critics broke away from their accepted conventions and modes to form a group of directors with an independent style of filmmaking in alignment with their belief that a film is personal; a mode of artistic expression carrying the mark of its creator(s).

Characteristics of New Wave Cinema

Their innovative style relied on experimentation in set design, decor, lighting, camera work, unusual depictions of space, costumes, and makeup that together comprised the *mise en scène* of films.[1] The following distinctive traits characterised this fresh new style of experimental cinema:

- The films were shot on location rather than in studios.
- Handheld cameras were used to achieve extraordinary, often exaggerated angles, and there were frequent long takes, rapid cuts, and freeze frames.
- Live sound and ambient light were used without making adjustments in the studio.
- There was an emphasis on plot ellipsing. Elliptical editing is a technique used in film editing that allows shortening on-screen the duration of real-time events of a story. It is done through 'jump cuts' in which two sequential shots are taken from slightly different camera angles to give the effect of swiftly moving forward in time.
- The plot was deemphasised and dialogues were improvised to mimic the natural way people talked. There were quick transitions between geographical locations, times, and eras.
- The new cinema focussed on the representation of everyday life and common social issues.

The style was radically different from the classic Hollywood style and suited the New Wave's need to make films quickly and cheaply without incurring the huge expenses of commercial films.

What were these avant-garde filmmakers hoping to achieve? Firstly, theirs was an approach to cinema in radical and conscious opposition to the linear and representational narrative style of commercial films. They showed a preference for the aesthetics of form over the familiar and popular organisation of the aesthetics of content and characters. The intention was often to subvert an audience from an easy-going acceptance of ordinary day-to-day reality to a shocked acceptance of alternative realities. They also showed indifference to interpretation. The ultimate effect was to deconstruct the narrative language that had evolved over the previous sixty years and create a reflexive cinema, or meta-cinema, whose techniques provided a self-critical commentary on its own making.

The *Cahiers* critics made the first films of the New Wave in 1956–57; dramatic short films, shot in 16mm and made for the consumption of the domestic audience. They also wrote extensively on film theory, trying to educate the highly discerning French public. These first New Wave films were all, in their distinctive ways, paradigms of the new cinema, and did surprisingly well, receiving both critical and commercial success. They inspired others within the French industry to emulate this exciting new style, which led to a veritable explosion of low-budget, stylistically experimental films made by film lovers with little knowledge or experience. Most of these ventures failed.

The New Wave movement only attained international prominence when François Truffaut, Jean-Luc Godard, and Alain Resnais, the three most vibrant representatives of the movement, produced their first epoch-making feature films: Truffaut's *Les Quatre Cents Coups* (The 400 Blows), Resnais' *Hiroshima, Mon Amour* (Hiroshima, My Love*)*, and Godard's *À Bout De Souffle* (Breathless).

Truffaut, Godard, and Resnais, along with Chabrol, Rohmer, Rivette, Varda, Demy, Malle, and a few others, were brilliant directors whose films tended to focus on family life and all aspects of man-woman relations in contemporary France, particularly Paris and its suburbs. Their films were shot on location and reflected the mannerisms and colloquial habits of common people. Godard's use of slang and swear words in *Breathless*, for instance, rang wholly true even though they proved offensive to the general audience. What characterised these films was a focussed gaze on the everyday familiar realities of French life centring around its cafes, bars, residential apartments, and shops rather than the 'larger than life' subjects that held the commercial films together.

François Truffaut went on to make commercially successful films such as *Les Quatre Cents Coups*, (The 400 Blows) in 1959, which was the first in the 'Antoine Doinel' series, *Tirez Sur Le Pianist* (Shoot the Piano Player) in 1960, *Jules et Jim* (Jules & Jim) in 1962, *L'Enfant Sauvage* (The Wild Child) in1970, *La Nuit Américaine* (Day For Night) in 1973, and *Le Dernier Métro* (The Last Metro) in 1980. Then there were his homages to Alfred Hitchcock, *Mariée était en Noir* (The Bride Wore Black) in 1967, and *Vivement dimanche!* (Confidentially Yours) in 1983.

Jean-Luc Godard made stylistically unique films such as *Une Femme est une Femme* (A Woman Is a Woman) in 1961,

Alphaville in 1965, *Pierrot le fou* in 1965. He directed several films on political and social themes from a Marxist or even Maoist perspective, such as *Le Petit Soldat* (The Little Soldier) in 1960, *Vivre Sa Vie* (My Life to Live) 1962, *Les Carabiniers* (The Riflemen) in 1963, *Bande à Part* (Band of Outsiders), 1964, and *Weekend* in 1967, among others. His provocative features include *Sauve Qui Peut (la vie)* (Every Man for Himself) in 1980, *Passion* in 1982, *Je vous salue, Marie* (Hail Mary) in 1986, and *Éloge de l'Amour* (In Praise of Love) in 2001.

Alain Resnais's most famous film was the postmodern mystery *L'Année dernière à Marienbad*, (Last Year at Marienbad) in 1961, which explored the effects of time on human memory, a typical theme of Resnais's work. *Muriel* in 1963, *La Guerre est Finie* (The War Is Over) in 1966, *Stavisky* in 1974, *Providence* in 1977, and *Mon Oncle d'Amérique* (My American Uncle) in 1978, were some of his other films.

Claude Chabrol was a director from the original *Cahiers* group, who dedicated many of his films to Alfred Hitchcock, such as *Le Beau Serge* (Handsome Sarge, 1958), *Les Biches* (The Does, 1968), *La Femme Infidele* (The Unfaithful Wife, 1969), and *Le Boucher* (The Butcher, 1970), among others.

Louis Malle had a journalistic bent of mind and produced more than ten documentaries besides drama films, thrillers, and romantic comedies: *Elevator to The Gallows* (1958), *Murmurs of the Heart* (1971), *Au Revoir Les Enfants* (Goodbye, Children; 1987), *The Silent World* (1956), and *Atlantic City* (1980), to name a few.

Eric Rohmer, the elegant and erudite filmmaker, made a name for himself with films in three path-breaking series, with each being a portrayal of emotions and passions buried deep in the human consciousness. His first series of six 'moral tales' included *Ma nuit chez Maud* (My Night at Maud's, 1969) and *Le Genou de Claire* (Claire's Knee, 1970), while the second series of six films on comedies and proverbs showcased films like *The Aviator's Wife* (1981), *Pauline at the Beach* (1983), *Full Moon in Paris* (1984), etc., and finally the series on *Tales of the Four Seasons*: *Springtime, Winter, Summer, and Autumn*.

The widely acclaimed and awarded Agnès Varda's films had a distinctive experimental, almost documentary-like style, and dealt with feminist and other social issues: *La Pointe Courte* (1955), *Cléo from 5 to 7* (1962), and *Vagabond* (1985), for instance.

Jacques Demy had a childhood love for the style and sentiment of Hollywood musicals, which made him render the same in a French setting and create something magical with *Three Seats for the 26th* (1988), *The Pied Piper* (1972), *Lady Oscar* (1979), etc.

Jacques Rivette was another member of the movement, who became the editor-in-chief of *Cahiers du Cinéma* until 1965. Rivette made his abstract and experimental films under the mentorship of greats of the New Wave such as Truffaut, Godard, Rohmer, and Chabrol. *Paris Belongs to Us* (1961) was his first feature film, made with the initial support of Italian neorealist director Roberto Rossellini. Other films included *The Nun* (1966), *L'Amour Fou* (Mad Love, 1969), and *Out 1* (1971).

For many years after its launch in the early 50s, the French New Wave, spearheaded by the *Cahiers* group, held the lead as the harbinger of Modernist and Postmodern film and film theory. This small band of sophisticated and talented filmmakers dominated French cinema until well into the 1970s and 80s, and several continued to make significant contributions even into the next century. But come the 1990s, France along with other European countries, began to succumb to market pressures just like the rest of the world, and the influence of the New Wave started to wane. Under the increasing demands of the box office, filmmakers turned gradually to crime thrillers, period films, and mythological costume dramas–genres that especially caught the fancy of young directors wanting to make commercially successful films.

In conclusion, it must be said that no national movement influenced international cinema as strongly as the French New Wave did. Its directors used films crafted into 'novels' and 'essays' so to speak; as an audio-visual language to communicate thoughts, feelings, and experiences, as well as to educate. By deconstructing classic Hollywood conventions, they added dimensions to this language that made it capable of expressing a whole new range of internal emotions and external behaviour.

Influence of the New Wave in Neighbouring Countries

American directors, Irvin Kershner (*A Fine Madness*, 1966), John Frankenheimer (*Birdman of Alcatraz*, 1962), Robert Altman (*Countdown*, 1967), Arthur Penn (*Bonnie and Clyde*, 1967), Stanley Kubrick (*2001: A Space Odyssey*, 1968), and Sam Peckinpah (*Major Dundee*, 1965) used the camera and editing techniques of New Wave cinema to make films on politically and socially bold, often subversive, themes. Frankenheimer's *The Manchurian Candidate* was a political thriller about communists brainwashing American soldiers, and Stanley Kubrick's *Lolita*–an adaptation of Vladimir Nabokov's novel of the same name, dealing with the uncomfortable subject of the incestuous and paedophiliac obsession of an older man for a twelve-year-old stepdaughter–was made in the mode of a satirical black comedy.

New Wave cinema also manifested itself in countries across Europe. In Germany, a new generation of filmmakers made feature films that dared to take a closer look at the country's unhappy and 'unassimilated past'. Three such influential figures of the German New Wave movement were Rainer Werner Fassbinder (*Fox & His Friends*, 1975; *Ali: Fear Eats the Soul*, 1974; *Eight Hours Don't Make a Day*, 1972), Werner Herzog (*Wodaabe: Herdsmen of the Sun*, 1989; *Bells From the Deep*, 1993; *Cave of Forgotten Dreams*, 2010), and Wim Wenders (*The Goalkeepers Fear of the Penalty*, 1972; *Paris, Texas*, 1984; *Wings of Desire*, 1987).

The Czech New Wave (1962–68) also called the 'Czechoslovakia film miracle', boasted of an impressive line-up of directors such as Miloš Forman (*Black Peter*, 1964), Věra Chytilová (*Daisies*, 1966), Ivan Passer (*Intimate Lighting*, 1965), Pavel Juráček (*Case for a Rookie Hangman*, 1970), Jiří Menzel (*Closely Watched Trains*, 1966), Jan Němec (*Diamonds of the Night*, 1964), and Jaromil Jireš (*Valerie and Her Week of Wonders*, 1970) among others.

Roman Polanski of Poland (*Rosemary's Baby*, 1968);

Miklós Jancsó, András Kovács, and István Szabó of Hungary; Aleksander Petrović of Yugoslavia; Bernardo Bertolucci, Marco Bellocchio, Ermanno Olmi, Pier Paolo Pasolini, and Francesco Rosi from Italy; and Bo Widerberg and Vilgot Sjöman from Sweden, made films in the idiom created by the New Wave.

In Britain, inspired by the French Nouvelle Vague, a group of young directors in the 60s, such as Karel Reisz, Jack Clayton, John Schlesinger, and Lindsay Anderson made films out of real stories, highlighting the struggles of the working class. Tony Richardson and John Osborne, two other well-known names associated with the British New Wave, explored socio-political developments within the country. Their films bore a close kinship with movements associated with art, literature, and theatre.

New Wave cinema from Asia that reached international audiences during this period was widely acclaimed for its freshness and experimental techniques, even though it faced disapproval from home audiences because of its controversial subjects. Many of the films coming out of China, Taiwan, and Korea ultimately had to go 'underground' for fear they would be subjected to government restrictions and end up being communist propaganda films. We must not forget that the year 1949 was also the year of Chairman Mao's communist revolution in China.

Despite the repression of their creative outflow, there were a few talented young directors in Hong Kong, such as Tsui Hark, Ann Hui, and Patrick Tam, who challenged the film industry norms of the country, giving birth to the Hong Kong New Wave in 1979. In Taiwan, young directors such as Edward

Yang, Te-Chen Tao, I-Chen Ko, and Yi Chang contributed to what came to be known as New Taiwanese Cinema. Their films differed vastly from the melodramatic kung-fu action films of Taiwan's earlier eras and came to be hailed instead for their realistic, down-to-earth, and sympathetic depiction of life in urban or rural Taiwan. These films were compared stylistically to the films of the Italian neorealism movement.

The Korean New Wave, from the late 1990s to the present, produced both of the country's highest-grossing films, *The Admiral: Roaring Currents* (2014) and *Extreme Job* (2019), as well as prize winners on the festival circuit including Golden Lion recipient *Pietà* (2012) and Palme d'Or recipient and Academy Award winner *Parasite* (2019).

Nagisa Oshima of Japan was a legendary New Wave filmmaker who was counted as equal to Godard, or perhaps even more influential than the French master. His films dealt with politically controversial themes (*Night and Fog in Japan*, 1960), *Crime and Punishment,* (*Death by Hanging*, 1968; *Boy*, 1969), and the taboo subject of sexual desire in all its manifestations (*Diary of a Shinjuku Thief*, 1968; *Gohatto*, 1999). He, and others like him who defined the New Wave, were influenced by the internationally famed filmmakers among them: Akira Kurosawa and Kenji Mizoguchi.

Indian New Wave

The Indian New Wave emerged in the decade between 1970-80 as a natural upshot of the Parallel Cinema movement of the 1940s and 50s, which had been initiated in Bengal by Satyajit Rai, Mrinal Sen, and Ritwik Ghatak.[3] The authors of Parallel films, or Art films as they were also called, were heavily influenced by the formal and thematic characteristics of Italian neorealism–factuality, naturalism, symbolism, and an intent to depict the socio-political realities of the times. This can be said of all in the group except Ritwik Ghatak, who broke from realistic cinema to make more formalised and stylised, metaphysically abstract films.

Even though both sobriquets, 'new wave cinema' and 'art film', are often interchangeably used when discussing parallel cinema in India, there were stylistic differences between the two kinds of films. They each had their own distinctive conventions though both were subgenres of new experimental cinema. Even though Mrinal Sen (*Bhuvan Shome*, 1969) was commonly hailed as the pioneer of the New Wave in India, it was Mani Kaul who was the first to usher in radical experimental cinema into the country with *Uski Roti* (Our Daily Bread, 1969). It was a film that displayed a unique aesthetics and grammar different from all established norms of filmmaking. For all purposes therefore, Mani Kaul is the avant-garde flagbearer for the new cinema that broke into the Indian scene in the late 1960s.

Kaul was impressed by the works of Robert Bresson and followed his minimalist style. He did away with music and used austere settings and elliptical editing to elongate the passage of time. *Uski Roti* was based on Mohan Rakesh's short story of the same name. Set in rural Punjab, the film focuses on Balo, a young wife, waiting by the roadside to hand her truck driver husband, Suchcha Singh, his lunch packed in a tiffin box. The movie was neither meant to entertain nor to tell a story. It offered instead a unique cinema experience. The film was multi-layered with complex visual imagery, using the surrounding landscape as a metaphor, with minimal dialogue, unusual camera angles, and a slowed pace typically characteristic of the New Wave.

The story of the Indian New Wave started with the government of India setting up the Film Finance Corporation (FFC) in 1960 to provide funding to talented filmmakers from the Film Institute of India and outside of it, who wanted to make socially meaningful films but could not afford the costs of big-budget commercial films. With the assistance of the FFC, the first films of the Indian New Wave rolled out in the year 1969–Mani Kaul's *Uski Roti* (Our Daily Bread), Mrinal Sen's *Bhuwan Shome* (Mr Shome), Basu Chatterjee's *Sara Akash* (The Whole Sky), and Kantilal Rathod's *Kanku* (which was made in Gujarati).

While *Uski Roti* was almost entirely in the genre of experimental cinema (The pace is extremely slow, there is a great amount of emphasis on foreground imagery such as the hands, eyes, and facial expressions, and there is little or no dialogue to carry the story forward), *Bhuwan Shome*–a satirical comedy on the petty corruption in the railways and the loneliness of an upright railway officer–had more of a story and more clearly delineated characters. So did *Sara Akash*, while delving into the intricacies of the relationship between a husband and wife and their reluctance to adjust. The camera in *Sara Akash*, wielded by the talented cinematographer, K. K. Mahajan, pans through the streets of the town in bold sweeping shots, then turns to show the claustrophobia of a young bride who finds herself confined to the constricting spaces of a crowded new home, within the walls of which the newlyweds must establish an intimate relationship. It captures with unusual candour the inner stifling of all of young Prabha's dreams and desires as she endures the indifference her husband shows towards her as she is engulfed by loneliness. The eponymous *Kanku*, a film adapted from Pannalal Patel's Gujarati short story of the same name, is about a young village belle Kanku, who loses her husband while she is pregnant. It follows her subsequent struggles with loneliness and longing and her eventual succumbing, despite initial resistance to an illicit sexual encounter with the village grocer.

Kumar Shahani (*Maya Darpan:* Mirror of Illusion, 1972), Avatar Kaul (*27 Down*, 1974), M.S. Sathyu (*Garam Hawa:* Scorching Wind, 1973), Shyam Benegal (*Ankur:* The Seedling, 1974), Saeed Mirza (*Albert Pinto ko Gussa Kyon Ata Hai*, 1980), and Govind Nihalani (*Ardh Satya*, 1983) in Bombay, and G. Aravindan *Kanchana Sita* (Golden Sita, 1977), Adoor Gopalakrishnan *Swayamvaram* (Choosing a Husband, 1972), and Girish Karnad, *Kaadu* (The Forest, 1973) in the south, were the other important filmmakers of the New Wave. Most of them had trained in film schools and their films were offbeat, technically sophisticated experiments in style, form, and camera work. Shot in real locations, the films had new and fresh faces rather than established actors to tell their tales of everyday life. The directors dispensed with any kind of linear plot or narrative, or fractured realistic depictions, and used elliptical editing to create elongations over time.

Most of these films were also adaptations of literary works, novellas, short stories, and plays, another typical feature of new cinema. *Sara Akash*, for instance, was based on the first part of Rajendra Yadav's debut novel *Sara Akash* (The Infinite Cosmos), and *Bhuwan Shome* was based on a Bengali story by Balai Chand Mukhopadhyay. *Maya Darpan* was an adaptation of Nirmal Verma's short story by the same name. Avatar Kaul's *27 Down* was based on the Hindi novel by Ramesh Bakshi, *Athara Sooraj Ke Paudhe*, which narrated the story of a railway employee who meets a girl on a train. *27 Down* was the only film made by this talented filmmaker who met with an untimely death due to an accident after the film was released.

Even though there was immense variation in the style, content, and aesthetic sense of each filmmaker, they were bound together by common intent. They sought to use the medium to the best effect, aiming to portray the human predicament—a human being's sense of isolation, and his hopeless search for identity, some sort of stability, and companionship. All this as he finds himself drowning in a sea of contradictions, weighed down by the ambiguities, insincerities, and chaos of the real world. These filmmakers were also bound by the desire to expose the brutal manifestations of the social mores prevailing around them. Knowing the impact of films on the Indian public imagination to be enormous, they attempted to shape people's understanding of issues such as gender inequality, poverty, social injustice, caste, and marginalisation of sections of the population. And there was one common trait—they consciously and unanimously rejected the formulaic approach of songs, dances, comic interludes, and fight sequences that defined conventional Bollywood films.

The cinematic innovation and technical experimentation of New Wave cinema helped constitute a body of extremely impactful work that held sway for a period of time. But its influence began to lessen after a decade or so with the resurgence of commercial culture, with formula films making a comeback. With two of Bollywood's cult films, Ramesh Sippy's *Sholay* and Yash Chopra's *Deewar* arriving on the scene in 1975, the tide began to turn against realistic socio-political films with a human angle. The script and dialogue writers for both *Sholay* and *Deewar*, were the writer duo Salim-Javed. Skilfully combining the merits of Indian gangster films and spaghetti westerns, *Sholay* turned out to be a slickly made revenge drama against an idyllic rustic setting, a grand spectacle of daredevil action, dance, music, comic relief, and the oomph of the film's well-endowed female lead. The fact that it failed to deal with socially relevant issues did nothing to lessen the film's appeal. *Sholay* ran with packed houses for months, going on to become the highest-grossing Hindi film at the Box Office ever (counting inflationary changes).

Deewar was a crime film loosely based on real-life smuggler Haji Mastan's life story. Both *Sholay* and *Deewar* featured Amitabh Bachchan as the male lead and did wonders for his career as they wrought magic at the box office. A new and more polished sort of formula film had emerged that would rule in the decades to come.

With the arrival of such films, realistic cinema rapidly began to lose the power to draw crowds. Many actors such as Om Puri, Naseeruddin Shah, Smita Patil, and Shabana Azmi, who had made significant contributions to these films and had acquired critical acclaim for their roles both nationally and internationally, moved to the commercial stage for more lucrative work. Parallel cinema began to lose patrons and support from financiers and film distributors. In the words of Ira Bhaskar,

> Lack of distribution and exhibition, and hence an inability to reach its audiences and a consequent financial non-viability, may have destroyed the New Wave movement by the mid-1990s, but it has nonetheless left an important legacy of cinematic innovation and experimentation. Perhaps there is a genealogy here for the new, edgy experimental cinema of today.[4]

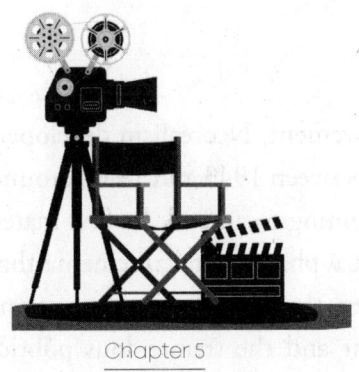

Chapter 5

Cinematic Reflections on Reality:
Realism and Neorealism

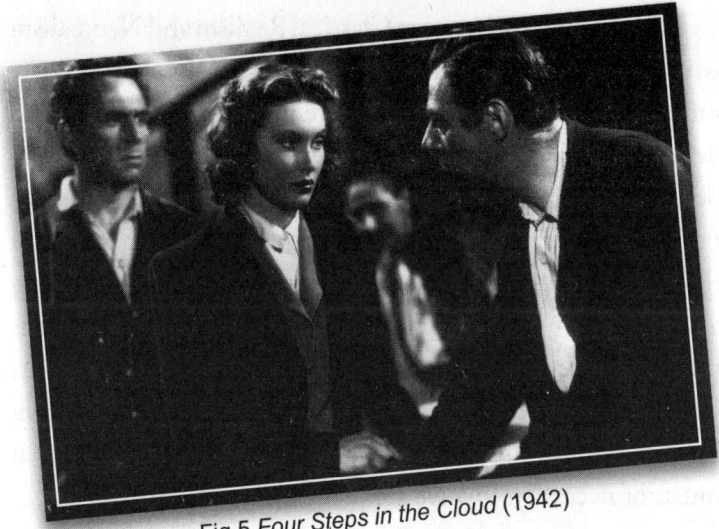

Fig.5 *Four Steps in the Cloud* (1942)

AS a film movement, Neorealism developed in diverse parts of the world between 1943 and 1945, around the time World War II was coming to an end. Its first materialisation was in Italy, marking a phase in Italian cinema that coincided with a period when the country was transitioning through the ravages of war and the tremendous political upheaval that followed in its aftermath. Though it started more as a trend presaging the New Wave movement in cinema rather than a new school of cinema produced by a group of like-minded directors and scriptwriters, it had an enormous impact not only on the future of Italian cinema but also on the French New Wave and subsequently on cinema across the world.

The distinction between Classical Realism and Neorealism is important. Realism in cinema was neither a genre nor a movement specific to a time; there were no fixed criteria to define its subject matter or structure. Cinematic Realism can be best understood as opposed to fantasy. Realism does not fictionalise truth, seeking instead to give a faithful account of things as objectively as possible, using sound, camera, editing and other techniques of filmmaking. Some might say this is impossible, as cinema, by nature, is a medium that presents its subject matter in a way designed to please, entertain, inform, educate, or influence audience behaviour. Thus, it must, of necessity, involve some dressing up of truth.

Whichever way one looks at it, Realism serves as an important reference point in discussing the nature of cinematographic images and their credibility, the relation of film to reality, and the role of cinema as a novel way of understanding the world.

Realist films have a documentary feel in that they have raw aesthetics, starkly depicting reality in sordid detail. They focus on the perceived world and the natural meaning people give to what they perceive.

Yet Realism does not simply point to that which is realistic. While offering a criterion of assessment for judging how close cinema comes in its representation of some or other, often neglected, aspect of human reality, it also describes a complex relationship between reality, the film, and the audience, which shifts like quicksand according to the subjective cultural preferences of the audience. Reality is as much shaped by our objective perception of 'what is', as by our subjective desires and our urge to see 'what could be'; to look at facts in one way rather than another.

Realist cinema deemphasises any grand telos or purpose to human life, treating human beings as selfish creatures inhabiting a far-from-perfect world. It deals with humdrum reality and tries to show that there is nothing uplifting about ordinary human experiences. It also deflates the importance of canonical ethical values as dogma. Instead, it sees moral norms as no more than functional codes of conduct created by popular consensus according to general convenience to achieve certain selfish human ends.

Italian Neorealism – National Cinema

Neorealism, on the other hand, describes a specific movement in cinema and a definite style of filmmaking that differed from previous forms of film Realism, both stylistically and technically. As André Bazin, a French film theorist and critic, argued in his book *The Evolution of the Language of Cinema*, 'Neorealism portrays: truth, naturalness, authenticity, and is a cinema of duration'.[1] The necessary characteristics of neorealism in the film have been defined as follows:

- A definite social context
- A sense of historical actuality and immediacy
- Political commitment to progressive social change
- Authentic on-location shooting as opposed to the artificial studio
- A rejection of classical Hollywood acting styles; extensive use of non-professional actors whenever possible
- A documentary style of cinematography

Early Neorealist cinema in Italy took the form of fictionalised documentaries–hybrid films that wove real-life incidents into a tale of love or valour.

Alessandro Blassetti's *Four Steps in the Cloud* (1942), a film about the lives of ordinary characters from the working class; Augusto Genina's *The Siege of Alcazar* (1940), a nationalist propaganda film for the fascist regime in Spain in the form of a documentary, romanticising and celebrating General Franco's infamous defence of the fortress in Toledo during the Spanish Civil War; and Mario Camerini's *What Scoundrels Men Are!* (1932), a comedy film about Bruno–a chauffeur with problems keeping a job–meeting a taxi driver's daughter working at a perfumery as a shop assistant, and his trying to impress her by pretending to be rich; these were some of the best specimens of Italian Neorealism in its formative stages. Cesare Zavattini is another name associated with this early phase. Zavattini, who was the movement's primary scriptwriter, theorist, and spokesperson, worked with many celebrated directors of Italian and international cinema to produce some of the masterpieces of early Neorealism. For instance, *Sciuscia* (Shoeshine, 1947) starring Vittorio De Sica (who later shot to fame as a director with his film *The Bicycle Thieves*), and Genina's *The Siege of Alcazar* (1940), were films that heralded the post-war Neorealist movement in Italy and embodied the classic features of the genre.

However, it is Luchino Visconti's *Ossessione* (1942), based on James M. Cain's novel *The Postman Always Rings Twice*, that is considered by many to be the first Neorealist film. It tells the story of Gino, a drifter who finds himself at a diner/gas station one night, where he meets Giovanna, the young wife of the owner Bragana. A disgruntled Giovanna, now fed up with the dreary work at the diner and her life with the equally dreary Bragana, seduces Gino and gets him to help her murder her husband. Besotted with Giovanna, Gino agrees, and the couple engages in a crime that leads them into a sordid dance of betrayal and death. The film was suppressed by the fascist censors. Another of Visconti's films, *La Terra Trema* (The Earth Trembles, 1948), is a meticulous depiction of a fisherman and his family's struggle to overcome poverty and exploitation. Shot entirely on location in a

Sicilian fishing village, the film is regarded as a brilliant piece of Neorealist cinema.

However, De Sica's 1948 film *Ladri Di Biciclette* or *The Bicycle Thieves*, is perhaps the best representation of Italian Neorealism. The tale is typical of Neorealist cinema. Antonio Ricci, playing the protagonist Lamberto Maggiorani, is a common man who, after years of searching, has finally found a job posting movie posters across the city. As the job is dependent on his having a bicycle, Maggiorani and his wife Maria pawn their bed sheets to be able to buy back his bicycle from the pawn shop. However, in a pathetic turn of events, his bicycle is stolen on the very first day of work. Ricci and his son Bruno then proceed on a seemingly never-ending search for the thief and the bicycle. The film ends without the father-son duo ever finding either.

The tale is about an ordinary citizen's helplessness at being suddenly deprived of a possession that is key to his livelihood. The entire cast of the film was made up of ordinary people who had never acted before. The shooting took place in actual Roman locations without glamour or embellishment. The cinemagoer only sees dirty old buildings with windows missing glass in their frames, streets empty without the bustle and noise of vehicles but filled with people on foot wandering in search of work or other ways to earn money.

From a social perspective, the typical themes of this genre of films were the everyday struggles of ordinary folks; the daily toil of the humble working class, the abject conditions under which the poor lived, the brutal structures of subjugation, the exploitation, the oppressive orthodoxies of tradition, and regressive customs that kept them captive and tainted their relationships. Alternatively, the films focussed on the grim realities of war and its aftermath.

From the perspective of aesthetics, Neorealist cinema was identified by its rejection of the make-believe theatricality of commercial films, shot in artificially constructed studio settings with plastic characters strutting through improbable situations and accomplishing impossible feats. Instead, Neorealism tells stories from a human angle, seeking to capture ordinary events in a nation's history through narratives that are unembellished and uncontrived. Cinematic Realism is combined with social, political, or economic themes and the films don a stark look and feel, with sparse aesthetics and characters that almost elide into the ambient spaces, the landscape, the objects, and the furniture. There is an emphasis on natural sounds and musical scores are sparingly used, if at all.

Italian neorealism was a post-war movement that, like the French New Wave and German New Cinema that came after it, started as a form of national cinema, representative of the culture of the country from which it emerged–Italy. The major figures associated with the Neorealist movement had studied at Mussolini's Centro Sperimentale, the National Film School of Italy.[3] They crafted vivid and realistic modes of describing true incidents in the nation's history or told socially relevant stories about poverty, inequitable distribution of wealth, or social injustice. They shot in actual locations, using newsreel footage whenever possible, and featuring real people or nonprofessional actors.

These filmmakers turned away from the fascist-sponsored national cinema when they recognised it for what it was, a propaganda medium with a nefarious political purpose, foisting the government's agenda on its people. National cinema anywhere is government-sponsored. It is used ostensibly for nation-building by representing the nation to its people in the form of a definite identifiable space bound by finite boundaries and inhabited by a tightly knit, coherent, and unified community. This idea of nation and national identity is sought to be communicated through cinematic images, narratives, and music. The agenda is the homogenisation of its people, but fashioned as it is, out of a complex mosaic of frequently conflicting cultural constructs of language, race, ethnicity, religion, social class, gender, and sexuality, a common national identity is hard to forge.

For international audiences, their first introduction to the Neorealist movement was through Roberto Rossellini's *Roma, Citta Aperta* (Rome, Open City, 1945), a film that was shot on location in the streets of Rome, within two months of Italy's surrender to the Allied forces. Featuring professional as well as nonprofessional actors, it focused on the dilemmas of ordinary people caught up in extraordinary events. Its documentary texture, post-recorded soundtrack, and improvisational quality became the hallmark of the Neorealist movement.

Rossellini also made *Paisan* (1946) and *Germany, Year Zero* (1947) in this genre. Other major Italian Neorealists included:

- Vittorio De Sica (1901-74): *Umberto D.* (1952) was an important film central to the movement. De Sica exercised considerable influence on Indian filmmaker Satyajit Ray (*Pather Panchali*)
- Federico Fellini (1920-93): *La Strada* (The Road, 1954), *La Dolce Vita* (The Sweet Life, 1960), *Nights of Cabiria* (1957)
- Michelangelo Antonioni (1912-2007): *Chronicle of a Love Affair* (1950), *The Cry* (1959), *L'Avventura* (The Adventure, 1960), *The Passenger* (1975)
- Giuseppe De Santis collaborated with Luchino Visconti on the script for *Ossessione* but made his directorial debut with *Caccia Tragica* (Tragic Hunt), a film dealing with an appeal for better living conditions for the Italian working class, as well as corruption, the black market, and the treatment of erstwhile soldiers. De Santis's third film *Bitter Rice* (1950), the story of a young woman working in the rice fields, was a landmark Neorealist film that fetched De Santis an Academy Award nomination for Best Original Story.

These were individual filmmakers who had their unique styles and visions. Most of them were young filmmakers making their first feature films around this time. A moment in history had brought them together over a common interest—making films on lean budgets that necessitated avoiding expensive studio setups and shooting on location, showing everyday realities and people's personal experiences rather than the stylish phantasms of commercial films. They focused on making a comment on the social and sexual mores of the times without artifice to a discerning audience, working without using a pre-planned script or sophisticated camera work.

The second generation of Italian directors who emerged after them, namely, Pier Paolo Pasolini (1922-75), Ermanno Olmi (1931-2018), Bernardo Bertolucci (1941-2018) and the still-living Marco Bellocchio (1939), followed the standards of the Neorealist model—long camera shots to capture the texture of a setting, actual locations, non-professional actors, using the city or village space as a character, natural lighting, and post-synchronised sound in their films.

Neorealism in France and Other Countries

Jean Renoir, the precursor of Italian and French Neorealism, was the son of the Impressionist painter Pierre-Auguste Renoir. His two films, *La Chienne* (The Bitch, 1931) and *La Nuit du carrefour* (Night at the Crossroads, 1932), which represented the genre with their take on the grim realities of life, were produced when he was already nine films old. Renoir came to be known for the keen human eye with which he approached his subjects, placing people at the centre of everything and creating deeply sensitive, astonishingly beautiful cinema, both silent and with sound.

Renoir went on to make films on social issues—*Boudu sauvé des eaux* (Boudu Saved from Drowning, 1932), an adaptation of Gustave Flaubert's classic novel *Madame Bovary* (1934); *Toni* (1934), a realistic story of Italian immigrant workers; *Le Crime de Monsieur Lange* (The Crime of Monsieur Lange, 1935), a political film encouraging collective action against capitalist corruption, and *La Vie est à nous* (The People of France, 1936), a propaganda film for the French Communist Party containing a blend of both fictional elements and documentary footage. Two pre-World War II films, *La Grande Illusion* (Grand Illusion, 1937) set in a World War I prison camp, decrying the utter futility or the 'grand illusion' of war, and *La Règle du jeu* (The Rules of the Game, 1939), saw Renoir portraying the angst of a civilisation being crushed under the weight of conflicting classes and national identities. In a society overtaken by an obsession with 'social manners' to the exclusion of real emotions, Renoir makes a passionate appeal for preserving the sanctity of human relationships. The films are considered masterpieces, both thematically and technically.

Renoir's experiments with cinema techniques such as sound and deep-focus cinematography earned him international regard.[3] His influence reached deep into Hollywood and can be seen in films that were produced after he had immigrated to America in 1940, in a bid to escape Nazi persecution.

Renoir and Jacques Prévert's 1936 film *The Crime of M. Lange*, is considered by many to be one of the most important French films of the time and an essential part of a film studies curriculum anywhere. It is known for its beauty, spontaneity, and wit, as well as for its astute understanding of the political realities of a nation. The film's left-inspired theme, relating to the conditions of a 'popular front' against the privileged class and the establishment of a workers' collective, was meant to foster an overall spirit of resistance against Nazism. At the same time, it tells a highly entertaining romantic story about its zany but lovable mix of eccentric characters going through a gamut of extreme situations. Renoir and Prévert's film was as creative as the culture of which it was a product. It held a special appeal for the common man as it reflected their ordinary experiences in a manner that they related to, which helped the film to give tough competition to the glossy theatrical releases of the day. Finally, the film is also a study of film aesthetics with its clever use of image, narrative, and diegetic storytelling.[4]

After its release, the Communist Party asked Renoir to make propaganda films explicitly denouncing fascism, a request with which Renoir was happy to comply as he was convinced that it was every French citizen's duty to resist Nazism.

Renoir is often identified with what is known as Poetic Realism, a film movement in France in the 1930s. It is defined as follows,

> Poetic Realism films are 'recreated Realism'...They usually have a fatalistic view of life with their characters living on the margins of society, either as unemployed members of the working class or as criminals. After a life of disappointment, the characters get a last chance at love but are ultimately disappointed again and the films frequently end with disillusionment or death. The overall tone often resembles nostalgia and bitterness. They are 'poetic' because of a heightened aestheticism that sometimes draws attention to the representational aspects of the films.[5]

The Neorealism movement influenced the films of Satyajit Ray in India, Akira Kurosawa in Japan, and directors in Germany,

Spain, and Eastern Europe. But, with the socioeconomic reconstruction of Europe taking hold in the 1950s under the impact of the bold Marshall Plan that aimed to push back the spread of communism, Neorealism's role as a propaganda vehicle began to wane in Europe. Italian Neorealist cinema nevertheless remained prominent through the films of several gifted directors who began their careers as Neorealists and went on to produce their major work during the 1960s and 70s.

Art Cinema

Neorealism morphed into Art cinema around this time. In a strict sense, the term art cinema refers to a strand in European cinema that emerged in the 1950s, setting its high artistic standards to coincide with the modernist traditions fashionable in other forms of twentieth-century art.

Art cinema's narrative and textual qualities were distinct from that of the 'drama-action-plot-melodramatic acting' schema of popular cinema put out by Hollywood, Bollywood, and production houses across the world. Conventional cinema had linear narratives with definite endings, predictable plot lines, and sharply delineated black-and-white characters. Its appeal being mass-based, it displayed a common filmmaking style with conventional camera work and editing. Art films, on the contrary, were auteur pieces bearing a strong, identifiable authorial mark–they were traceable to the director. Though thematically broad, they could be identified by their 'realist' project, as they tended to delve into the drama of human existence, exploring the psychology and the existential problems of intuitive, suffering human characters, in a stark minimalist style. In that sense, they were the centrepieces of the critical discourse around cinema art.

A marked fact about art-house cinema was that films in this genre were characteristically screened at outlets other than commercial cinema circuits, adhering to specialised exhibition venues such as film clubs and societies, and dedicated repertory cinemas. They were generally meant for the consumption of the wealthy intellectual elite whose tastes identified with 'high culture'. The ciné clubs in France, Germany, Great Britain, and the US were exclusive venues for screenings of foreign films, experimental films, and avant-garde films. Elsewhere, film festivals became popular locations where art films were screened.

Indian Neorealism

From its early inception, the Indian film industry has had a staggering rate of film production, at times topping 2000 feature films per year, and eclipsing Hollywood in the process. Many of these films are so mediocre that they sink without a trace. But the 1930s saw a shift when the major studios across the country: Mehboob Studios, Bombay Talkies, and Ranjit Movietone in Bombay, New Theatres in Calcutta, Prabhat in Pune, and the studios in Madras began to show a keen interest in making films that were not run-of-the-mill 'masala' movies but represented parallel cinema about progressive social themes. There were several directors even within the mainstream Bollywood film industry, who evinced interest in making more meaningful films, including Mehboob Khan, Guru Dutt, V. Shantaram, Raj Kapoor, and Bimal Roy.

The period between the 1930s to 1950s is considered the golden age of Indian cinema. It was an age when these legendary filmmakers pioneered films of a different flavour and outlook, focusing on human relationships and the human condition, and taking a close and critical look at Indian society's middle-class values. Many of them, like their associates in the film industry, had arisen from the rank and file of the lower and upper middle class, and their experiences informed the films they made. Filmmaker Mehboob Khan, the son of a police constable from a village in Gujarat, started as an extra in silent films and made his way up to open a production studio of his own.

His films–*Aurat*, remade years later as *Mother India*, *Humayun* (partially recovered from archives), *Roti*, and *Amar*– were dedicated to Realism. Raj Kapoor, who was hailed as the greatest showman in the history of Indian cinema, came from an upper-middle-class family of film folks who emigrated from Pakistan to India after the Partition. Raj Kapoor was inspired by the three Italian greats, Rossellini, De Sica, and Zavattini, with whom he came in close contact while they were in India for the 1952 Bombay Film Festival. This brief association led him to make his first film *Aag* (1948), followed by *Barsaat* (1949), and *Awara* (1951) in the Neorealist style.

Guru Dutt, Bimal Roy, and V. Shantaram likewise came from upper caste lineage but modest economic backgrounds. Their forte was romantic-realist melodramas that highlighted important social issues, advocated humanism, and yet remained entertaining. For V. Shantaram, the film medium was an efficient instrument of social change. His films, *Jhanak*

Jhanak Payal Baaje (1955), *Do Aankhen Barah Haath* (1957), *Navrang* (1959), and later *Pinjra* (1972), were successful films that exposed the rampant bigotry and injustice of a caste-ridden Indian society. Guru Dutt was a master of mood and lighting. His three broodingly dark films–*Pyaasa* (1957) and *Kaagaz ke Phool* (1959), both with Dutt as director and actor, and *Sahib Bibi aur Ghulam* (1962) as producer and actor–won him international recognition. Bimal Roy's *Do Bigha Zameen* (1953), *Parineeta* (1953), *Madhumati* (1958), *Sujata* (1959), and *Bandini* (1963) were beautiful gems of realistic cinema. They had simple dialogues and soulful music with evocative lyrics written by lyricists who came from humble backgrounds. Shailendra, who wrote most of the haunting melodies in Bimal Roy's films for instance, was a 'fitter' at a workshop in the Indian Railways; and Hasrat Jaipuri, who along with Shailendra wrote the immortal songs in Raj Kapoor's films, was a bus conductor.

Satyajit Ray and Ritwik Ghatak

In Bengal, Satyajit Ray and Ritwik Ghatak, who came to be identified as the master craftsmen of Neorealism or art cinema, came from upper middle class, educated, and well-off Zamindar families, and therefore had the leisure and opportunity to dabble in artistic pursuits.

Satyajit Ray's father Sukumar Ray and grandfather Upendra Kishore Roy-Choudhury were well-known illustrators and authors of children's books. They translated the Ramayana and the Mahabharata and authored the children's magazine, *Sandesh*. Thus, Ray too began his professional life as a commercial artist in Calcutta (now Kolkata).

He warmed to the Apu story when he was commissioned to illustrate editions of two Bangla novels, *Pather Panchali* and *Aparajito*, by Bibhuti Bhushan Bandyopadhyay (which later provided the source material for his films). But the actual inspiration for making a film version of the stories came from Jean Renoir, who was in India for a brief period to film his movie, *Le Fleuve* (The River, 1951).

While helping the great director scout for locations, Ray was encouraged by the former to make a film of his own. The idea coalesced in his mind when Ray went to London on a tour and binge-watched films including some films of Charlie Chaplin, and Vittorio De Sica's Neorealist masterpiece, *Bicycle Thieves*. De Sica's film gave Satyajit Ray the artistic model he had been looking for. Both Renoir and De Sica exercised a profound influence on all of Ray's work thereafter. Jean Renoir became his mentor and remained a major inspiration throughout his career.

The Apu Trilogy – A Study in Neorealist Aesthetics

Pather Panchali (Song of the Little Road) in 1955, was Satyajit Ray's first feature film, followed by *Aparajito* (The Unvanquished) in 1956, a film that took up Apu's story from where *Pather Panchali* had left off. In 1959, he followed up with the last film in this set, *Apur Sansar* (The World of Apu), which completed what is known as the Apu trilogy. The three films are considered classic examples of Neorealist cinema from India.

Pather Panchali begins with Apu's birth in a Brahmin family that lives in abject poverty, in a village bordering the woods somewhere deep in the interiors of rural Bengal. The father, Harihar (Kanhu Banerjee), is a scholar and playwright who finds himself at odds with his doltish neighbours because of his education and his calling as a writer and poet. Even though Harihar is unable to provide for the most basic needs of the household, for there is no money to be made through learning, he retains a trusting and cheerful outlook on life. With his infectious optimism, Harihar makes a constant effort to prop up the drooping spirits of his wife, Sarbajaya (Karuna Banerjee), who has lost hope of ever seeing her family rise above their circumstances. Sarbajaya's character is very prominent in the first half of the film. She is shown as a severely proud and strong-willed woman who has conservative social expectations. She reposes a desperate faith in her husband, but with him being absent from their home for long periods, she finds herself swinging between her two neighbours, one of them a kind-hearted soul who helps her with food and sometimes money, and the other who is quarrelsome and mean.

Amidst such pathetic circumstances, we find Apu and his mischievous doe-eyed older sister Durga, growing up as happy children. Apu constantly follows Durga (Uma Das Gupta) around while she is frequently seen being chastised by annoyed neighbours for stealing fruit from their orchards. Their grandmother, a toothless hag, bent over with age but with a robust appetite, totters around the family home, cackling and grumbling and constantly threatening to leave when she feels unacknowledged and neglected. Chunibala

Devi, in the role of a lifetime, delivers a brilliant performance, easily the best in the entire film.

In the time it takes for Apu to grow into a gangly, wide-eyed lad of seven, Satyajit Ray walks the viewers through a series of carefully designed, yet completely artless, depictions of village life. Skilful camera work and sound are used to advantage, aiding the great director in portraying meanings well beyond what the scenes capture. There are moments of great poetic beauty in the film when the narrative comes to a halt to allow the camera to play with the surroundings, and music to infuse the viewer's senses. There is a long sequence in which the old grandmother is sitting outside with the evening shadows growing long, singing a mournful folk song in her cackling quavering voice. The camera circles her, closing in on her creased and warped body and her toothless face which is yet so expressive and beautiful. Another long shot of a flying insect skimming over the water's surface transfixes the viewer to a timeless moment.

Apu (Subir Banerjee) remains mostly silent, struck with fascination and wonder at everything he sees. He attends school in a dirt-floored, open-walled shelter that doubles up as a classroom and grocery shop. We see him playing with his sister and with the other children, envying the relative prosperity in which some of them live. Apu and Durga never tire of exploring the village and the bordering woods. The camera closes in often on the overgrown vegetation, the tangle of roots and branches, water puddles along the footpaths, and the delightful little clearing in which the children play their childish games, trying to imitate the events of adult life. It is where the village girls gather surreptitiously to make the modest homely *khichuri*, with Durga describing the essential ingredients and the girls eating it with relish. The scene where Durga is eating tamarind and occasionally letting her brother lick the sour and gooey mess of her fingers is beautifully crafted, bringing the viewer close to the experience of the salivary glands bursting as the sharp tangy taste of the tamarind hits the tongue. Ray uses scenes such as this to effortlessly convey the small pleasures that punctuate the lives of simple folks.

There is an iconic sequence in which the children are seen trekking a long distance from home to watch a train drawn by a steam engine, belching smoke and hurtling through the fields. As Apu and his sister gawk at this wonderous phenomenon, the expressions on their little faces inscrutable, the viewer is hit by the incongruity of modern machinery tearing asunder an idyllic rural setting.

As the film inches towards its climax, we see the father leaving home in search of work, and the mother forced to cope with starvation. The grandmother dies and a storm reduces the humble family home to shambles. The night of the storm makes a devastating statement about the defeat and despair staring at the family. Even the idol of the Lord Ganesh trembles at the force of the gale.

Young Durga catches pneumonia as there is no way to shelter from the driving rain, and no medicines to bring down the fever. She dies even as her mother frantically sends the young Apu scampering to fetch the kindly neighbour, in the desperate hope that her child might be saved. When the father returns and beholds the appalling destruction of his home and everything around him, the audience waits with bated breath for the moment when he must learn of Durga's death. It is a scene in which sound fades out entirely, leaving only Pandit Ravi Shankar's sombre notes to convey the father's wrenching, keening sorrow. There is an immediate audience connection as the grief that threatens to destroy him echoes the grief that would strike the heart at losing a loved child, whether that heart is a human's or an animal's.

Soon after, the family packs up what remains of their meagre belongings and prepares to leave for the city of Benares where the father must move to find work. In the penultimate scene, as the family is about to move, Apu finds the necklace that his dead sister had once stolen from her friend but never admitted to having done so. He takes it from the jar on a high shelf where she had hidden it and throws it into the pond near their home, in an action signifying that everything about the village, including its most sacrosanct memory of their beloved Durga, now sullied by the knowledge that she had been dishonest, must be left behind before they move. The camera lingers on the moss-covered surface of the water where the necklace has disappeared, but the moss has not quite closed over the spot where it had landed. There is a small circle that the necklace has cleared signifying that the village and the dead sister cannot be completely erased from Apu's psyche.

In *Pather Panchali*, the jungle is a character too, adding veracity to the story as it unfolds. It helps establish an intimate link between man and his environment. Ray uses long shots to show the jungle reverberating with its mysterious sounds amidst its equally mysterious silences. Human habitation is shown as having encroached into the jungle rather than the other way around. When the family packs up its belongings and leaves for the city, the wilderness is seen reclaiming what belonged to it in a brilliant scene showing the lithe form of a snake gliding into the ruins of the house.

In the second film of the trilogy, *Aparajito* (The Unvanquished, 1957), Apu and his family have moved to Benares where his father Harihar, becomes a priest carrying out his business on the banks of the Ganges. But Harihar dies soon after and his mother, Sarbajaya, is forced to begin work as a maid. As time passes, Apu and his mother, assisted by a great-uncle, manage to return to Bengal and settle in a village called Mansapota. There Apu apprentices as a priest but continues his studies at the local school where he excels at his studies and wins a scholarship that helps him to move to Calcutta in pursuit of further studies.

Though Sarbajaya is filled with trepidation, she allows him to leave for the city, packing his things for him with great care. But left all alone, Sarbajaya feels abandoned and yearns constantly for Apu's visits which become increasingly rare as Apu adjusts to city life and becomes distanced from his village roots. She falls sick but does not disclose her illness to Apu, for fear he may leave his studies and come back to be with her. When Apu finally learns of her illness, he rushes back only to find that she has died.

The extremely sensitive and authentic performance by Smaran Ghosal as an intelligent and sensitive Apu in his youth, helped the film win many an award. Especially poignant was his portrayal of Apu's restless mind, always hungry to learn new things and always curious to explore.

In the final film, *Apur Sansar* (The World of Apu, 1959) we have Soumitra Chatterjee playing Apu. The actor was a favourite of Ray who cast him in several of his films. Apu joins a friend at a wedding in the country, and when the groom has a mental breakdown and abandons the bride-to-be on the *mandap*, Apu is persuaded to marry the hapless girl Aparna (Sharmila Tagore) and save her from disgrace and the fate of dying an old maid. Apu returns to Calcutta with his new bride, dazed at the quick pace at which events have overtaken him. But even as the newlyweds are beginning to get accustomed to one another and love is born between them, fate deals a cruel blow. Aparna dies in her country home while giving birth leaving Apu grief-stricken. Finding it hard to cope with the loss of his wife and holding the baby responsible for her death, he abandons the newborn with its grandparents and goes wandering off. The film ends with Apu, who, having drifted aimlessly and in despair for five years, finally comes to his senses and goes back to the village to retrieve his son so that he can be a father to him.

The Apu films were not political, nor did Satyajit Ray intended his films to change social realities. One does not see any strong ideological position taken by the filmmaker, unlike his contemporary Ritwik Ghatak. Instead, Ray wanted to create individual characters that resembled ordinary human beings and situate their intertwining lives in a continuum of cinematic space and time. All of Satyajit Ray's films exuded a charm and vitality that drew the audience into an intimate bond with the characters. Ray made the viewer forget the narrative and contemplate the psychological complexities of human relations instead. Through his films, he explored an entire range of human emotions from joy, tenderness, and wonder, to loneliness, fury, anguish, and despair, all conveyed through the soft exchange of a glance, a quick averting of the face, an inscrutable expression, or intense brooding eyes that concealed more than they revealed. Ray would weave these disparate emotions into his characters in an almost banal manner to create the impression that these were all an integral part of life.

Like most Neorealist filmmakers, Ray made his films on a very low budget. It is said that Ray started *Pather Panchali* with his own funds, which soon ran out. He could go on to finish it only when the State decided to give him funding. Thus, there is a raw feel about the film which enhances its appeal. There is also a rawness to the soundtrack, even though Ravi Shankar's music provides depth and class to the background score.

Despite the budgetary constraints, the three Apu films are not crude and simple ethnographic works. Far from it. These are films of exceptional cinematic sophistication with intensely artful camera work and clever yet unobtrusive editing, comparable to a De Sica or a Rossellini. Like the Italian greats, Ray's Neorealism was not artless naturalism but a conscious application of cinematic tools to create a fascinatingly real and objective world. Satyajit Ray's films qualify as some of the best examples of both Realistic and Arthouse cinema just as did Rossellini's and De Sica's films.

Ray employed a carefully constructed style of filmmaking. In his films, we find Jean Renoir's technique of plugging in the minutest details into the surroundings and the ambience of a film and imbuing his character with several shades of complex emotions. Besides Renoir, Ray was also influenced by Federico Fellini with whom he shared his calling as an illustrator.

The landscape plays an important role in Neorealism. In *Voyage to Italy* (1953) not only are the cities of Naples, Capri, and Pompeii portrayed in great detail by Rossellini, but they are a part of the story itself, in some subtle way playing a role in undermining the marital ties between the two protagonists. Similarly, Ray's characters, whether in his rural films such as the *Apu* films or *Asani Sanket*, or his films about the city—*Mahanagar*, *Pratidwandi*, *Nayak*, *Jalsaghar*, *Jana Aranya*, *Seemabadhdha*, and finally *Agantuk*, blend into the surrounding spaces, their lives fused with the animate and inanimate surroundings. The surface of an algae-covered pond, a broken or bent-out-of-shape bronze bowl, water dripping from a faucet or a leaking roof, a broom standing against the corner, and the food on the table, all make the environment come alive, at the same time imbuing the narrative and the characters with meaning.

Ritwik Ghatak

The Bengali filmmaker Ritwik Ghatak was a contemporary of Satyajit Ray. Ghatak belonged to a family of rich landowners who migrated to Calcutta from Dhaka, Bangladesh, then East Bengal, after the catastrophic Bengal Famine in 1943. His father was a civil servant and a Sanskrit Pandit, and his niece, the daughter of his brother Manish Ghatak, was Mahashweta Devi, the famous writer. The childhood experience of loss and displacement as he and his family fled to Calcutta from the famine that engulfed rural Bengal left a traumatic impact on young Ritwik, but his experience of the horrors of partition as an adolescent boy in his twenties–a partition both of the country into India and Pakistan and his beloved homeland into East and West Bengal–scarred him for life. The films Ghatak made, eight features and several documentaries, bear the mark of his agony and angst. Ghatak turned to Marxism as he tried to make sense of the madness and mayhem of the communal riots post-partition. His films were intensely political, infused with his obsession with the communist ideology. Ghatak remained a communist all his life after having joined the CPI and its art and culture wing, the Indian Peoples Theatre Association or IPTA, in 1951. At the same time, he was also taken with the tenets of feminism. Many of his films depicted an idealised womanhood that was commodified and exploited by a highly patriarchal Indian society.

Ritwik Ghatak's films include his first film *Nagarik* (Citizen; completed in 1952 and released in 1977), followed by *Ajantrik* (Pathetic Fallacy, 1958), *Bari Theke Paliye* (Runaway, 1958), and the renowned partition trilogy, *Meghe Dhaka Tara* (The Cloud-capped Star, 1960), *Komal Gandhar* (E Flat, 1961), and *Subarnarekha* (The Golden Thread, 1962). All his films bear the stamp of his own life experiences. His disenchantment with the Independence of the country, which promised deliverance from British rule but tore the country in two, forms a refrain in the Partition trilogy. Similarly, his engagement with feminism guided his visualisation of the persona of his three heroines in these films, Nita in *Meghe Dhaka Tara*, Ansuya in *Komal Gandhar*, and Sita in *Subarnarekha*, in meticulous detail. The three women embody the loss and desolation of partition and convey his anger and frustration at the pretence and futility of Indian nationalism. In a later film of his, *Jukti Takko Aar Gappo* (Reason, Debate and a Story; 1974), Ghatak himself plays the protagonist, a nervous and alcoholic intellectual who travels around the countryside meeting people and listening to their unique life stories. In another, *Titash Ekti Nadir Naam* (A River Called Titas; an Indo-Bangladesh outing in 1973), his exploration of the lives, loves, and deaths of his characters who are all fisherfolk who live along the banks of the Titash river in Bangladesh, is awash with his nostalgia for the Bengal of his lost childhood, and the sorrow which remains always fresh in his heart.

Ghatak's films displayed many elements of Neorealism. He shunned the studio setup and moved out into the streets and gullies of the city, discarded script, avoided design, and used trained actors only sparingly, if at all. The audience viewed the waking life of his characters as though they belonged in the same frame.

Yet it is not easy to situate Ritwik Ghatak in that tradition. His films used 'melodrama' which is a modern style different from Neorealism, requiring the elements of the film to be pitched more forcefully and more loudly than realist cinema allows. Even though, like Ray, the immediate context of his films was the everyday struggles and dreary lives of the lower strata of the middle-class feudal society, Ghatak portrayed his characters as long-suffering victims of the system and added the cultural nuances of leftist radicalism, something Satyajit Ray steered clear of. Ritwik Ghatak's films make an overtly political statement about the monumental tragedy of the partition of India; the disintegration of identities and personal histories among a people displaced from their roots.

Both he and Ray are filmmakers who took an unambiguous moral stand against the follies, injustices, and exploitative atrocities of their society. But the latter's films are more immaculate and better-planned, in which personal stories and elements of history are interwoven. Satyajit Ray's films are more introspective; about individual conflicts. Ghatak's films are disjointed, riven with moments of anguish and alienation, saturated with his great sense of disorientation, anger, and disappointment at having to leave his motherland, his beloved East Bengal. A style distinct from Ray places him among the auteurs of Indian Cinema.

While Ray's films went on to do commercially well and earned acclaim both at home and abroad, commercial success eluded Ritwik Ghatak. His films did not do too well at the box office except *Meghe Dhaka Tara*, and it has been alleged that his films were sabotaged by people who did not approve of his communist leanings. Some of Ghatak's films were too obscure to even aspire for commercial success. *Ajantrik*, an adaptation of a story by Subodh Ghosh about a man and his relationship with his broken-down taxi, along with his first film *Nagarik*, did not find an audience at home, apart from the most die-hard cineastes. Satyajit Ray's films found influential patrons who have ensured that they are well preserved for posterity, but Ghatak's films have languished mostly in his ancestral home, unheeded and uncared for. Without intervention from the government or some wealthy connoisseur taking control, Ritwik Ghatak, the master filmmaker may pass into oblivion.

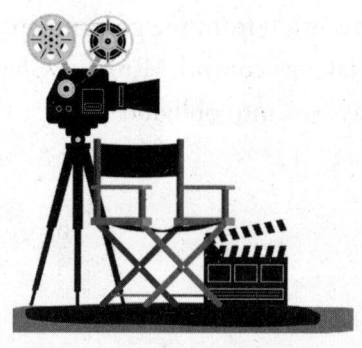

Chapter 6

Deciphering the Unknown:
Dealings in Documentaries

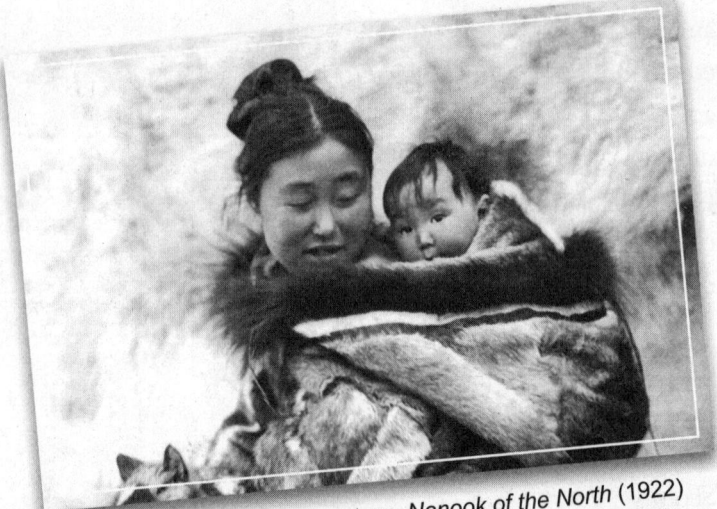

Fig.6 World's first documentary- *Nanook of the North* (1922)

Defining the Documentary

THE Oxford English Dictionary gives the following definition of a documentary, 'A documentary film is a non-fictional, motion picture intended to "document" reality, primarily for instruction, education, or maintaining a historical record'. Broadly speaking, a documentary is a non-theatrical film seeking to offer a non-fictional exposé of practices, histories, or cultures specific to a geographical region or milieu.

It is thought to have a social objective, among other things, creating an accurate understanding of a subject, guiding an inquisitive mind toward an unknown focal area and encouraging further exploration of the same. It informs, educates, sensitises, and motivates people to take corrective action against an undesirable or unjust state of affairs. Being non-theatrical, documentary films are peculiarly suited to promote understanding and dialogue on diverse matters concerning race, class, gender, livelihood, sexual orientation, communal relations, or a fading practice or institution.

The illustrious founders and proponents of the documentary film have defined it variously. For John Grierson, the founder of the Documentary movement in the UK, it is 'A creative treatment of actuality' and for Henry Forsyth Hardy, Scottish critic, writer, film administrator, and commentator, it is, 'A selective dramatization of facts in terms of their human consequences'. For legendary American filmmaker, photographer, art administrator, and author of documentaries such as *The Photographer* and *The Skyscraper,* Willard Van Dyke, the documentary is, 'A film usually non-fiction, in which the elements of dramatic conflict are provided by ideas and political or economic forces'. Speaking about his foray into the genre, fuelled by an early interest in photographing things connecting with social issues (as in his portraits of migrant workers), Van Dyke said, 'I was young and impatient, and felt that the documentary film would more effectively communicate issues to more people than would still photography'.

Paul Rotha, another leading British documentary filmmaker and a film studies writer from the early 1900s, a period when the documentary film industry had just started to grow, said, 'Documentary's essence lies in the dramatization of actual material' and 'Documentary must be the voice of the people speaking from the homes and the factories and the fields of the people'. According to John Marshall, 'The distinction between theatrical and documentary film is that the consequences for their words and actions are real for the people in the documentary; they cannot pick up their pay checks and go home when the shooting stops'. Well-known French film director Jean Benoit Levy stated, 'Documentary films are those which reproduce life in all of its manifestations—the life of man, of animals, of nature—without the assistance of professional actors or studios and on condition that the film represents a free artistic creation. We are led to name this genre *films of life*'.

A more formal definition came from the Academy of

Motion Pictures, Arts, and Sciences: 'Documentary films are defined as those that deal with historical, social, scientific, or economic subjects, either photographed in actual occurrence or re-enacted, and where the emphasis is more on factual content than on entertainment'.

Identifying Characteristics

Over the decades, the term has branched off into several sub-categories making it difficult to present an easy classification. Yet the following may broadly be laid out as the predominant features of a documentary film:

- Unlike a fictional film, the subject matter of documentaries is factual, dealing with things as they are in the real world—the nature of objects, practices, or institutions, and events impacting an individual, a race, a society, or a civilisation.
- Its primary aim is not to provide an art experience; rather it is to inform and/or educate, create interest, promote understanding, and encourage dialogue or reformative action in a wide variety of contexts.
- Documentaries are usually shorter in length than feature films and require shooting on location. They display a representative rather than a creative form. The film footage is captured from actual locations without any added dressing and with real subjects, whether people, animals, natural imagery, or events, who are unselfconscious and unmindful of the camera. Often the camera may be hidden, unobtrusively recording what people do and say.
- Documentaries capture reality in a manner that is

immediate, without needing any mediation of script.
- Documentary films were originally shot on 16mm film, a format that dominated moviemaking from the 1920s to the 1990s.[1]

A Brief History

The documentary as we know it today evolved into a distinctive film type in diverse regions of the world, post the Second World War, most prominently the US, Great Britain, France, Germany, and the Soviet Union. Much before that, it also had a noteworthy presence in the form of short, single, or two-reel films in several countries, including India, which has always been a major hub for films of all kinds.

One of the first documentaries to be made was *Nanook of the North* (1922), a naturalistic dramatization of the idyllic way of life of the Eskimos. This film was made by the legendary American explorer and filmmaker Robert Flaherty (1884-1951), hailed as the father of the documentary film in America. Flaherty grew up in Canada, exploring the country's vast sub-Arctic regions with his camera and keeping photographic records of indigenous populations he encountered and the inhospitable terrains he traversed. For *Nanook of the North*, he lived with the Eskimos for over sixteen months, recording their lives on reel. The film became an international success, setting global standards of excellence for nonfiction filmmaking.

John Grierson, a Scottish filmmaker in the 1930s, founded the documentary movement in Britain. It was Grierson who coined the term 'documentary' while reviewing *Moana* (8

February 1926, New York Sun), Robert Flaherty's fictional documentary film on a family from a Samoan village on the South Seas, uncorrupted by civilisation.

Grierson was reconceptualising the notion of creativity when he described the documentary as a 'creative treatment of actuality'. He believed that a film that had materials 'taken from the raw', with real people and real scenes rather than fictionalised accounts and actors, defined an art form in itself. He also believed that a film that 'documented reality' in this way, had a social responsibility toward reinforcing the democratic norms and practices of a society. Grierson's film *Drifters* (1929), about the North Sea herring fisheries, was internationally acclaimed as defining the genre of what is called social action documentaries, promoting awareness about social institutions such as class and labour. The film is also an account of modern industrial society.

Flaherty's and Grierson's films were silent black-and-white films.

In the world's first communist country, the Soviet Union, short educational films (often single reels) and newsreels were the earliest documentaries made in the 1920s, with the primary purpose of educating the masses on the ways, means, and aims of communism. A newsreel is a short documentary film, containing news stories and items of topical interest. Newsreels were prevalent between the 1910s and the mid-1970s as a source of information on current affairs. Many 'agitprop' films–short propaganda films–were made in the period after the first world war, to agitate or move the masses to participate enthusiastically in state-approved activities.[2]

The Battleship Potemkin directed by Sergei Eisenstein (1925), is considered one of the most important documentaries of all time. It was a dramatized account of the mutiny aboard the Russian battleship Prince Potemkin in 1905. Its importance lies in Eisenstein's use of cinema technique as much as its allegorical nature. Eisenstein made use of montages (not shots rolling one after the other but juxtaposed against one another with abrupt cuts) to make a film that cleverly fictionalised propaganda, showing the power of the masses grouping against the czarist state. The film was voted the greatest film of all time at the 1958 Brussels World's Fair Expo '58, but when *Citizen Kane* was released the same year, Eisenstein's film was dislodged from that position.

Man with a Movie Camera (Soviet Union, 1929), an experimental silent film directed by Dziga Vertov, is part documentary and part art cinema. It is a daylong, morning-to-night recording of life in a Russian city. Earlier, Vertov had made *Kino Pravda*, the well-known film about Russia in transition between the Bolshevik Revolution and the Civil War, between the 'Reds' and the 'Whites', which led to the establishment of the Soviet Union. In *Man with A Movie Camera*, the director uses a variety of complex and innovative camera shots, sans titles or running narratives, to celebrate the marvels of the modern city with its enormous buildings, dense population, and humming industries. The film defined a sub-genre of the documentaries of those times—the so-called 'city symphony' films that meticulously detailed the splendid exteriors and sleazy underbellies of modern cities.[3]

The documentaries that emerged out of France and

Germany in those early post-war years were realistic depictions of life and events in a specific period, sans all fictionalisation or dramatization. Cavalcanti's 'city symphony' *Rien Que Les Heures* (France, 1926), is said to have inspired Vertov's *Man with a Movie Camera* and Walter Ruttman's *Berlin: Symphony of a Great City* (Germany, 1927). The French and German 'city symphonies' showed the realities of daily living without romanticising like the American filmmakers, spouting social arguments like the British, or running propaganda like the Soviet documentaries. They used refreshing cinematic techniques combined with music and imagery to make their documentaries assume the form of unique art.

The legendary French filmmaker Alan Resnais' first project was to document the entire oeuvre of Vincent van Gogh's paintings. He did not seek to intersperse the paintings with shots of real fields of poppies or vases of flowers or night skies, the popular subjects that Van Gogh chose, as would have been expected. The paintings were abstractions of the real, and Resnais's film was realism once removed as it ranged over the real paintings of Van Gogh, without his camera for a moment leaving them.

The Subcategories of a Documentary
Television Documentaries
Radio and television forever changed the way documentaries are made. The two mediums provided a vastness of reach that was never before experienced. They allowed the filmmaker to enter people's homes, drawing rooms, and bedrooms. A whole gamut of themes came under the domain of documentary films, spanning

populations, social issues, personalities, events, practices, crime, war, drug abuse, international or national political events, race, gender, class, history, the market, and most prominently nature, her processes, phenomena, and inhabitants.

A difference between the classic documentary and the television documentary is that the former had its origins in motion pictures while the latter has its genesis in radio. A signifying characteristic of a television documentary is its adherence to a time slot. Every television documentary must adhere to the time allocated to it, whether a half hour or an hour, without considering if that amount of time is adequate for its subject.

Hybrid Documentaries

Documentary filmmakers whose business it is to represent reality in a non-fictional manner often use features and techniques of fiction films to introduce a touch of theatricality into the film; to assume the stance of a storyteller and thereby convey the theme of the film more effectively. The result is what is called a hybrid documentary. Hybrid documentaries experiment with mixing elements such as dramatized recreations, actors rather than real people, animation, innovative photography, music, and special effects with the typical features of the non-fictional documentary style of filmmaking such as actual interviews, archival footage, and observation cinematography (cinema verité methods) in the most fascinating ways.

Docudrama and Docu-fiction

A docudrama is a hybrid documentary that dramatizes

history in the form of a story; quite simply presenting truth in the form of fiction. The term refers specifically to telefilms or other television or radio media recreations that play up real events with the help of actors, interspersed with actual footage or recordings of the events themselves. The purpose is an alternative presentation of history that is informative while also being entertaining.

Many docudramas are feature-length films of more than two hours. *Killing Veerappan* (2016) is a Kannada-language docudrama written by K. Balaji and directed by Ram Gopal Varma. With a running time of more than two hours and twenty minutes, the film is about Operation Cocoon, which was launched by the Government to capture the famous sandalwood smuggler dead or alive. Anurag Kashyap's *Black Friday* (2004), based on Hussain Zaidi's 1993 book *Black Friday: The True Story of the Bombay Bomb Blasts*, is another Hindi-language feature-length docudrama with a running time of over two and a half hours.

Docufiction is somewhat different from docudrama. It is a more generic term that was recently introduced to signify a film genre that mixes fictional elements with real-time events and social issues, filmed as they play out. Docufiction is today a widely accepted category for the classification of documentaries on an international platform.

The Mock-documentary or Mockumentary

A mockumentary is a film or television show that depicts fictional events in the style of a documentary. These productions use the documentary format to recreate historical events at a later time or to deliver satirical commentary on contemporary happenings and issues by creating a fictitious setting for the same.

The Mondo Film

The Mondo documentary film, which originated in Italy, is considered one of the most controversial film genres of all time. Loosely translated Mondo stands for 'World'. The genre was invented by Italian filmmakers Gualtiero Jacopetti, Franco Prosperi, and Paolo Cavara, who jointly wrote and directed the first film of this genre, *Mondo Cane* (A Dog's World, 1962).

Mondo documentaries, also called shockumentaries, are a kaleidoscope of scenes in Technicolor; scenes of strange and shocking cultural practices from around the world; of forgotten tribes interspersed with scenes from modern city life that are so shocking as to provoke a collective gasp from the audience. The real-life and sometimes staged scenes mark the most depraved and bestial side of human beings. The film carries the descriptive tagline 'Tales of the Bizarre: Rites, Rituals, and Superstitions'.

In one scene of *Mondo Cane*, it is the early 1960's and a group of young men are taking part in strange rituals in the province of Castellaneta, Italy, to commemorate Rudolph Valentino, the infamous Italian actor from Hollywood, at his birthplace. Horrific scenes of ritualised suicide by Buddhist Monks are strung along with scenes of young sex-crazed girls from New Guinea chasing after men. On the French Riviera, a group of blonde women in ultra-revealing bikinis spy a ship carrying US sailors and begin teasing them from a distance by blowing kisses, sticking out their tongues, and displaying their bare breasts. A restaurant in New York serves sautéed butterflies, stuffed beetles, and fried insects flavoured with sauce, and in Formosa (Taiwan), dogs are grown, butchered, and skinned alive for dog meat, which is considered a portion of local gourmet food. In the streets of the big city of Hamburg, the dregs of society are seen strolling about in a drunken stupor while in another big city, Hong Kong, adolescent young girls are seen essaying into the night on their sampans (wooden boats) to sell their virginity to the highest bidders.

Mondo Cane spawned a host of pseudo-ethnographic films from the same genre in and outside Italy during the 60s. It came at a time when people were tired of black-and-white realist documentaries about some 'drab' aspect of real-life following the path carved out by the New Waves. They were eager to grab at every opportunity to give up the charade of being civilised and succumbing to guilty and long-repressed pleasures, even if second hand, and through a prurient viewing experience.

The audience of a Mondo documentary is conceived as voyeurs salivating in secret while they are being served platterfuls of truly bizarre happenings. As one of the great chroniclers of this epoch, J.G. Ballard observed, 'What the Mondo Cane audiences wanted was the horrors of peace… but they also wanted to be reminded of their complicity in the slightly dubious process of documenting these wayward examples of human misbehaviour'.[4]

The Mondo film is considered to have influenced many unsavoury aspects of contemporary culture including sensationalist news reportage, song albums with lewd and violent lyrics, reality TV, online child pornography, atrocity videos, and much more.

Documentary Films in India

In India, documentary films began to be produced in a systematically planned manner post-independence, when Prime Minister Jawaharlal Nehru recognised their potential as a medium of mass communication that could be harnessed for the leadership's nation-building efforts. Documentaries became powerful tools of state propaganda and were used to educate the masses on diverse subjects such as health and hygiene, farming, and formal education, while at the same time aiming to forge a strong national consciousness that would bind the diverse population into one nation. Earlier, the British government had made use of documentary shorts to propagate its war message. The leadership of the newly independent India took its cue from it when in 1948, Nehru instituted a government body called the Films Division with the express purpose of controlling the production and distribution of documentary films in India.

As early as 1896, a large number of short single reel films known as 'topicals' were being made by enthusiastic filmmakers acting independently, amongst whom were names such as Harishchandra Sakharam Bhatwadekar (fondly called Save Dada), Jamshed Framji Madan, and Hiralal Sen. However, once the FD was in place, it began producing its short films in the form of official documentaries. These were didactic and determinedly moralistic in tone and content, trying to ram information down the throats of viewers. The FD-produced documentaries had to be screened in halls each time before a full-length feature film could be shown. Unfortunately, these films were so boring that people would often simply wait outside the theatre for the entire duration of the documentary show, being able to tell from the signature tune when it came to an end, after which they would troop back for the main film. In an interview, an Indian researcher of filmography, Virchand Dharamsey, or Dharamsey Bhai as he is popularly known, says, 'People were compelled to see these films, but their duration was fixed and the music easily recognisable, so one could easily wait outside until the screening of the feature film. Some of these documentaries were as long as fifty minutes'.[5]

In the decades between 1948 and 1975, the FD churned out films promoting the vision and policies of the ruling party and its leader. A specific number of films were planned each year, and associated bodies were formed to work alongside the FD, including a Children Film Society (1955), the FTI or the Film Institute of India (1961), which is now FTII (Film and Television Institute of India), and the FFC (Films Finance Corporation). There were mainly seven kinds of documentaries produced by the FD:

- Experimental films and art films on subjects such as Indian arts, crafts, and cultural heritage. For instance, M. F. Hussain's award-winning film *Through the Eyes of a Painter* (1967), was commissioned by J.S. Bhownagary, who was then with the FD.
- Biographies, for example, Satyajit Ray's *Rabindranath Tagore* (1961) and S.N.S Sastry's *Portrait of a Prime Minister* (1974)

- Education films on farming, or skill-based instructional films
- Children's films including cartoons with morals
- Films for the promotion of export and tourism
- Feature-length documentaries
- Films on visits of foreign dignitaries

In the meantime, there were also private documentary filmmakers, both Indian as well as international, who had begun making short films that were not quite in line with the views and policies of the establishment. Their subject was often the excesses of the state, the pathetic economic conditions of ordinary people, and the far-reaching social inequalities and unjust practices that permeated the country. Avant Garde filmmakers such as S.S. Sukhdev with *India '67, Nine Months to Freedom, After the Silence, Khilonewala* and *Maa Ki Pukar*;[6] S.N.S. Sastry with films such as *And I Make Short Films* (1968, 18 minutes) and *Flashback* (1974, 21 minutes);[7] and Pramod Pati with *Explorer* (1968), *Claxplosion* (1968), and *Trip* (1970), were legendary documentary filmmakers of this period. There was also Jean. S. Bhownagary, who, while being at the FD, made brilliant experimental short films.[8]

This period of creative output soon ended with the declaration of the Emergency in 1975. Strict control was imposed by the ruling dispensation over films if they deviated too far from the official line. *Doordarshan* took over from FD as the official organ of the state in charge of informative filmmaking and news programs.[9]

The Central Board of Film Certification, a government

body popularly called the Censor Board, was constituted under the 1952 Cinematograph Act, and entrusted with the job of passing a film for release in theatres. After seventy decades, it is still around doggedly trying to serve the original purpose. Since all members of this body are government appointees, films that are critical of the establishment, flout the so-called 'norms of decency', or 'go against the interests of society' are seldom passed or granted certificates without cuts. The CBFC demands cuts on just about anything that makes the government of the moment nervous, and their nerves are extremely fragile! Thus, a raised middle finger, scenes showing prostitution, swear words, sex, the modus operandi of criminals, criticism of the State, and casual use of the national flag are all taboo matters and a film in which any such scene features will not be passed by the Censor Board.

Documentary films in India are subject to the same censorship norms as feature films. Films produced under government control do not face problems, but it is difficult for Indian filmmakers who work outside of the government's system of production and distribution to display their films in theatres or reach audiences around the world especially since their films are political and critical. As a result, Indian independent documentary filmmakers often face censorship issues and find themselves engaged in an extended struggle against government control of distribution and financing networks.

A Word About the Vikalp Initiative

In 2003, independent documentary filmmakers locked horns with the FD over its announcement of a censorship clause for Indian films at the upcoming Mumbai International Film Festival for Shorts, Documentaries, and Animation Films (MIFF), 2004. The condition outlined was that no film could be entered into the festival without a certificate. The Campaign Against Censorship (CAC), an action platform created by more than 275 filmmakers of the independent documentary movement and others supporting freedom of speech and expression, got together in August 2003 and formed *Vikalp - Films for Freedom*, an initiative to fight against the censorship clause that had been introduced. The collective issued a statement which said,

> The attempt to gag films at MIFF is part of a larger emerging scenario of extreme intolerance in India. Documentaries are now being recognised as a form that has the potential of inspiring debate and thought among diverse audiences. Many documentaries reveal 'truths' that are uncomfortable for those in power or seeking power. In the coming years, we will probably witness more attacks on documentary filmmakers, and therefore if ever this is the time for us to respond to these challenges as a community.[10]

The Vikalp initiative received massive support from the filmmaking fraternity and the public and forced the FD to disguise their intentions and resort to covert ways of censorship. Many of the best films that had won awards at major international festivals were rejected at the MIFF due to their political themes–the riots in Gujarat, the Narmada Bachao Andolan, movements for Dalit rights, corruption in the government, and so on. A film could also be rejected if the government considered it to have inappropriate content. Thus, films dealing with alternate sexuality, sex workers' lives, or relationships outside of marriage often faced the axe under the moralistic attitudes of the government whose directives the censor board abides by.

A multipronged strategy was devised by the CAC collective to register their protest at this blatant stifling of creativity. Films that had already been selected by the organisers were withdrawn from the festival by their makers in support of the filmmakers who had been denied entry. Efforts were made to try and engage with various stakeholders, including the jury, the Ministry, and the organisers of MIFF, to demand an independent review committee to address issues. Advocacy and information campaigns were planned to raise awareness among international filmmakers and film festivals, and Girish Karnad stepped down from the MIFF jury in sympathy.

The most interesting and effective move by Vikalp was the organisation of a 'Protest Show', an alternative festival of around fifty-eight films that were screened in the avenue next to the official MIFF venue, with the screenings going on at the same time as the festival timings.

The Vikalp festival received the unstinting support of all independent documentary filmmakers who wished to resist censorship in all its forms. Filmmakers pooled Rs 1000 each to fund the event. It was inaugurated on the fourth of February, with a theatrical performance of an excerpt from Saadat Hasan Manto's *Safed Jhoot*, a scathing comment on censorship and corruption. It was directed by Ratna Pathak-

Shah and Naseeruddin Shah and performed by Jameel Khan. This was immediately followed by the screening of *Aamakaar* (The Turtle People) directed by Surabhi Sharma, who had withdrawn the film from MIFF in protest. The film ran to a packed auditorium.

The films were screened to a large and enthusiastic audience over six days (more than fifty hours of viewing, with screenings that continued from 10 am to 10 pm). The Vikalp venue also provided a space for interactive discussions between filmmakers and their audiences in a completely informal setting—people sat on mattresses and the discussions happened over tea and *batatawada*, a local Bombay snack.

Later, a panel discussion entitled *Resisting Censorship* was also organised, where the panellists were writer Arundhati Roy; editor of the Marathi daily *Mahanagar*, Nikhil Wagle; and Anand Patwardhan, a rationalist filmmaker whose films have always been at the receiving end of the censors' scissors.

Vikalp was more than a festival. It showed the way forward for responsible citizens to come together in defence of freedom of expression. It shone a critical light on the harm unnecessary censorship could cause. As it reinvents itself, Vikalp aims to transform into a sustained movement against archaic censorship laws, creating a platform for healthy discussion over the need for alternative documentary filmmaking and providing avenues for the marginalised voices of dissent.

Changing Trends in Indian Documentary Filmmaking

Documentaries in India have, over the years, transformed into a lively art form, generating debate and activism about some of the most urgent issues of society. Modes of storytelling are shifting from 'simply documenting' to creating aesthetically designed pieces with a purpose–to cause interventions and disruptions in archaic social institutions that are in urgent need of reform.

One of the most notable documentaries made in India in the last decade is *Rangbhoomi*, a biography of Dadasaheb Phalke, made by veteran film, television, and radio director Kamal Swaroop. He first made *Tracing Phalke 1870-1944* (May 2013) under the aegis of the FD, produced by an associated body, the National Film Development Corporation (NFDC). The film was based on his coffee table book by the same name–a compilation of quotes, scraps, sketches, movie clips, illustrations, photos, collages, and workshop recordings, all relating to Phalke's life, woven together with a carefully researched narrative that includes reminiscences, snatches of conversations, and Kamal Swaroop's ruminations about Phalke. The film was released on 3 May 2013, to coincide with the date when, exactly a hundred years ago, the father of Indian Cinema, Dadasaheb Phalke, released India's first film *Raja Harishchandra* in theatres.

Swaroop's second film on Dadasaheb Phalke, *Rangbhoomi*, was an eighty-minute documentary that premiered at the Rome Film Festival in November 2013, as India's competition entry. It was based on Phalke's semi-autobiographical satirical play by the same name. Dadasaheb wrote *Rangbhoomi* during a period when he had been disillusioned with the world of cinema and had withdrawn to Benares to take up theatre; the play is a reflection on the deteriorating condition of theatre in his time. The film is also about its own making, as well as a critical commentary on the relationship between theatre and cinema. It went on to win the National Award (*Swarna Kamal*–Golden Lotus) for Best Non-Feature Film of the Year 2013.

Rangbhoomi is a remarkable film in many ways. The film starts with a shot of a stage that is in the process of being prepared for a theatre performance. The filmmaker is himself seen spelling out instructions about the stage setting and characters while reading aloud portions from Phalke's text. He intersperses the reading with discussions about the nature of literature, theatre, and cinema, explaining how cinema differs from literature in that it objectively 'fixes' the meanings in a film while literature allows the reader to imagine the same from the written words.

As the film progresses, Kamal Swaroop reconstructs the Benares of Phalke's experience through a startling mix of oral narrative accompanied by a psychedelic and surreal montage of old photographs of Phalke and his team, interviews with actors, scenes from the hustle and bustle of the old city, people on boats, glimpses from inside a racing train, dark and narrow streets and alleyways, scraps of handwritten texts emerging from the background, stray sounds of dogs barking and the calling of peacocks, the chanting of sadhus, and the sound of an oar cutting through the waters of a furiously flowing Ganga. Invocations from Phalke's play and Swaroop's musings about Dadasaheb run simultaneously throughout the length of the film.

The film uses 'juxtapositions', a classic technique of documentary filmmaking.[11] There are shots of the director reading from the text of Phalke's play, for instance, juxtaposed with shots of his young team members appearing against different backdrops in Benares (most likely the very places which Phalke himself visited while conceiving and writing his play). There are images of great beauty–a peacock outlined against the sky–juxtaposed with images of shocking squalor and crumbling logs and shattered houses. At times, the imagery alternates between being blurred and coming into sharp focus, and one image dissolves into the next. There are long shots taken by Kamal Swaroop with a hand-held, digital camera as he visits the very places where the actual events happened during Dadasaheb's sojourn in Benares in that long ago past.

Meenakshi Shedde, a well-known film critic and curator from Mumbai who has done extensive work on current trends and the future of documentary cinema in India, describes in a riveting lecture, the themes, subjects, styles, and forms of the new films that currently populate the documentary realm.[12]

She observes that documentary filmmakers today are primarily focused on affecting change or at least creating a difference. She lists many recent films on issues that are of central concern for modern societies, and the multiple modes of storytelling documentary filmmakers are using to present these in impactful ways.

Gender

FTII alumna, Reena Mohan's 1988 English language mockumentary *Skin Deep*, explores how urban, middle-class women in contemporary India view their bodies. The film is shot as a feature-length documentary (docu-feature) in which interviews with various women are cleverly crafted into stories in the first-person about women's conflictual relationship with their bodies, their efforts at coming to terms with all sorts of insecurities regarding their physical appearance, and the forlorn longing to acquire quintessential feminine appeal.

The HBO documentary *Pink Saris* (made by British director Kim Longinotto under the WMM- Women Make Movies banner in 2010) and Nishita Jain's *Gulabi Gang* (co-produced by the Norwegian producer Torstein Grude at Piraya Film, 2010), are two films on the same subject, dealing with a fiery group of local women from Bundelkhand, a rural district in the Indian State of Uttar Pradesh, who join forces to combat violence against women.

The English-subtitled Tamil film *Invoking Justice*, directed by Deepa Dhanraj, is about Muslim women of Southern India protesting the reality of Jamaats (all male legal councils) settling family disputes by applying Islamic Sharia law, without allowing women to even be present at the hearing, let alone defending themselves. In rebellion, the women set up their own Women's Jamaat which then took on the corrupt male-dominated judicial system.

Caste

Anand Patwardhan's feature-length documentary, *Jai Bhim Comrade* (2011) is an exploration of caste, focussing primarily on the 1997 police killings of Dalits in Mumbai's Ramabai Nagar. The film has an unusual format, being a hybrid documentary.[13] It is a 'musical' with the narrative unfolding through Dalit music, protest songs, lullabies, and raunchy qawwalis. Many of the songs are of the Kabir Kala Manch, a local troupe of Dalit poets, lyricists, and singers intent on using their music to raise awareness about the oppression of Dalits. In 2013, Patwardhan's film was honoured by the Sheffield International Film Festival with an Inspiration Award, and in 2014, the Mumbai International Film Festival honoured the filmmaker with the V. Shantaram Lifetime Achievement Award.

Human Psychology

Abhay Kumar's *Placebo* (2014) is another hybrid film, combining animation with actual footage to promote an understanding of the extremely tragic subject of student suicides in India. His film is shot on the premises of the prestigious All India Institute of Medical Sciences (AIIMS), Delhi, and his protagonists are graduates of the Institute, labouring under the unbearable pressures of competing and excelling amongst peers who, considering the minuscule acceptance rate of the institution, are perhaps some of the smartest students in the country.

Gay rights activist and filmmaker Nishit Saran, who was tragically lost to the world because of a car accident at the young age of twenty-five, makes use of home videos while dealing with the sensitive issue of homosexuality in his film, *Summer in My Veins*, a short forty-one-minute documentary made in 1999. The film is about a young man (Nishit himself), who takes an HIV test after finding out that he has had unsafe sex with an HIV-positive man. As he awaits his test results, he decides to come out to his mother. Reminiscing about it later, Minna Saran, Nishit's mother, says, 'In *Summer in my*

Veins, Nishit filmed the moment when he told me about his sexuality, that he was gay. I do not think any other parent would have quite that kind of coming out moment, but in their way, our children are always talking to us, trying to tell us about their lives, even when they can't say it out in so many words. Sometimes it is us who cannot bring ourselves to listen, or to even realise that there is something in the minds of our children that they cannot share with us'.[14]

Ashim Ahluwalia's film *John & Jane* is an experimental hybrid film which uses a mix of observational documentary techniques and science fiction to capture the phenomena of call centres in Mumbai. Many people who work in these call centres get caught in the turmoil of a make-believe world in which they are made to give up their original identities and assume new ones so that they can deal better with their American clientele. They are trained to speak with an American accent and are shown Hollywood films to learn American mannerisms, pronunciation, expressions, and phrases. The employees, some of whom are in desperate need of financial support for their families, dream of a better life and start doing things to themselves such as colouring their hair blonde and changing their names to anglicized ones to find acceptance, but end up with a full-blown identity crisis instead, having lost their natural body language, their culture, eating habits, social and moral values and much more. Ashim Ahluwalia's film is informative, entertaining, and technically smart. It is shot on prime 35mm film with smooth tracking of motion with a Steadicam stabiliser and dolly shots throughout the film for good cinematic effect.

Women filmmakers of the likes of Shohini Ghosh (*Tales of the Night Fairies,* 2002), Madhushree Datta (*I Live in Behrampada,* 1993), Paromita Vohra (*Morality TV and the Loving Jehad,* 2007), Saba Dewan (*Dharmayudhha* (The Holy War, 1989), and Deepa Dhanraj (*Invoking Justice,* 2011) have produced excellent work, combing all the elements of a great documentary with sensitive insights on issues such as women's sexuality or the plight of Muslim women in India.

Innovative Modes of Documentary Filmmaking in Current Times
Informative and Performative Documentaries

Chi Lupo, literally meaning Honey-hunters, is a short twenty-six-minute documentary made by independent filmmaker Kezang D Thongdok. It records an ancient practice of the Sherpduken tribe of Arunachal Pradesh, residing in the state's West Kameng district. The camera follows the Chi Lupo or honey hunters going into the nearby forests at great personal risk to collect a special kind of honey, found only in bee hives hanging from rocky outcrops. According to Kezang D. Thongdok, very few honey-hunters remain in the business. 'With the advent of modernisation, honey hunting is rapidly fading away. Within three or four years, this unique practice will fade out. The young generation isn't interested in hunting and harvesting honey because it is rigorous work. This practice is under threat…That is why I thought it was imperative to make this film, documenting the last of the honey hunters', he said.[15] The documentary has an English narration, with music by the traditional Sherpduken folk singers. Even though *Chi*

Lupo won the best documentary award at the tenth Dada Saheb Phalke Film Festival Awards in 2020, its critical success did not translate into commercial success.

Documentary-to-Feature

A documentary feature is a nonfiction motion picture that deals with its subject creatively. It is usually more than forty minutes in length and is released in theatres. A documentary feature may carry real-life footage combined with fictional elements, employing various techniques of cinema such as still photography, animation, re-enactment, and the like. What makes it a documentary is its emphasis, which is on fact and not on fiction.

Some documentaries were later made into feature films by their makers. For instance, director Vidhu Vincent's Malayalam film *Manhole* (2014) is a remake of her award-winning documentary, *Vrithiyude Jathi* (Caste and Cleanliness), based on the lives of manual scavengers in Kerala. *Manhole* won her two awards at the twenty-first International Film Festival of Kerala (2016), Best Malayalam Film and Best Debutant Director.

Art Documentaries

These films represent a visual portrait of the world's greatest contemporary artists, allowing us a glimpse into their real lives beyond the world of art. Most of these documentaries were made quite recently and include street art documentaries, as well as films that follow some of the most renowned contemporary artists in all spheres of creative expression.

Video Installations

Video installations are digital experimental multilinear narratives that do not abide by the usual norms of filmmaking. Video installation artists create documentaries that represent information with a degree of plasticity, by changing the context of the display and transforming the genre. The format aims to incorporate audience interaction into three-dimensional spaces, first by animating the space by juxtaposing ordinary objects with real people talking about their lives and shared experiences. Secondly, it coaxes new audiences into the gallery by the sheer novelty of appeal. Developments in video technologies and the internet have enabled this format of documentary film to find a niche for itself.

Documentaries presented as installations use what is known as 'détournement' wherein a new form is created by 'hijacking' conventional media. Guy Debord describes détournement as the use of two separate elements that displace the original, or the re-use of elements of well-known media to create a new work with a different message.[16] Détournement is the French word for deflection, diversion, rerouting, distortion, misuse, misappropriation, hijacking, or otherwise turning aside from the normal course or purpose.

Massive amounts of video footage can be used in video installations, which is not possible with film or TV. Some important examples of this sort of 'art' are Bill Viola's multi-screened works,[17] Gillian Wearing's use of documentary style to make art,[18] or Ming Wong's exhibition, *Bülent Wongsoy: Biji Diva!* 2014. The last was a mixed media installation featuring videos, sound and light installations, a vinyl record and cassette covers, a cassette wig, photographs, and archival material.[19]

The Importance of Documentary Films

Today, a documentary film is not simply a journalistic depiction of reality. It has attained the stature of an art form in its own right because of its fresh aesthetics and innovative exploratory styles. A good documentary deep dives into the core of its subject in order to portray reality as authentically as possible, but at the same time it broadens the spaces around the subject, incorporating new dimensions and using technology to enhance the film's appeal. All the same while makers of theatrical feature films can fictionalise truth, a documentary filmmaker must never lose sight of a primary aim with which the word documentary is associated—throwing light on existing social, political, and cultural realities of a region or milieu. Documentary films are an effective mode of mirroring central issues and debates in both the national and international arena relating to race, class, geographical displacement and alienation, urban and rural woes, and/or other aspects of reality. They can promote understanding and dialogue at a location that is so critical for these debates—the education system. Inevitably, therefore, nontheatrical films have come to play a central role in scholarship and teaching.

Documentary as Art

We will have to reconceptualise the regular parameters by which we judge conventional art forms belonging to the realm of art proper such as music, painting, sculpture, dance, or literature, if we are to accommodate the documentary film in the same realm. John Grierson, a student of philosophy and the first one to have used the term documentary, conceived it as, 'a creative treatment of actuality'. In that sense at least, one can characterise documentaries as art. In one of his papers, Grierson writes,

> My separate claim for documentary is simply that in its use of the living article, there is *also* an opportunity to perform creative work. I mean, too that the choice of the documentary medium is as gravely distinct a choice as the choice of poetry instead of fiction. Dealing with different material, it is, or should be, dealing with it to different aesthetic issues from those of the studio.[20]

Documentary filmmaking requires a fine eye for camera angles and moving imagery. The filmed material is at the beginning an amorphous mass of photographic images, moving pictures, and other details of the world in which individuals find themselves situated. The documentary filmmaker must carefully select the most significant elements out of this flux and organise and manipulate them to create a meaningful representation of reality. This is what makes documentary filmmaking so similar to the creative process used by an artist.

With the enormous technological advances in video and audio of recent times, the art of documentary has transformed from the old grainy, black-and-white recordings of drab subjects to the present-day ultra-sophisticated pieces that compare at par with any manner of art. The boundaries between documentary and art have now become blurred and that has worked to the advantage of both cinema and art.

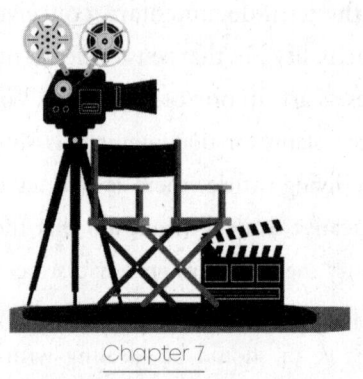

Chapter 7

Painting Gandhi on the Celluloid Canvas:
A Student Essay

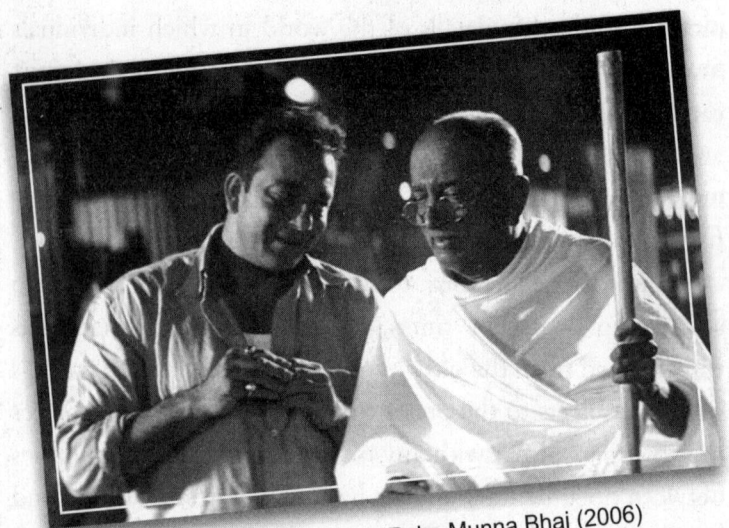

Fig.7 A scene from Lage Raho Munna Bhai (2006)

THE primary aim of this chapter is to critically analyse and evaluate a number of films made on Gandhi, and assess the accuracy and authenticity of their depiction of Gandhi and the values he stood for. Of them, Richard Attenborough's film, *Gandhi*, was selected as one of the best-known biopics on Gandhi, and Raj Kumar Hirani's, *Lage Raho Munna Bhai* for its attempt to popularise Gandhi through mainstream cinema. The reason for selecting movies like *The Legend of Bhagat Singh*, *Dr Ambedkar*, *Bose: The Forgotten Hero*, etc. for research is that the personalities on which these films were based were prominent leaders of their time, who worked along with Gandhi in the freedom struggle and ardently believed in ideologies similar to what Gandhi himself espoused. Gandhian philosophy is very approachable and relevant to all sections of society, and these leaders fought for the same ideals.

For the authenticity of facts and data reflected in the movies, we have referred to Gandhi's autobiography, *My Experiments with Truth*.

Depicting Gandhi's Personal Life in Cinema

Mohandas Karamchand Gandhi, also known as Mahatma Gandhi was a man of principle and discipline. The experiences he had in his childhood and other incidents of his personal life deeply influenced the manner of his participation in the freedom struggle. Not many films made about Gandhi have emphasised aspects of his personal life.

An interesting fact that emerged during our research is that the first documentary ever made on MK Gandhi was from before India's independence. A documentary, unlike a dramatization of an autobiographical subject, draws from actual footage of personal history. Impelled by his desire to make a film on Gandhi, well-known Tamil travelogue and journalist A. K. Chettiar travelled extensively throughout the country and abroad, collecting pictures and video footage of Gandhi's various action programs and speeches that had been stored in archives throughout the world.

He got around 50,000 feet of film out of all the data he had collected and began work converting the film footage into an eighty-minute documentary shot on 15 mm film. Started in 1937 and completed in 1940, the film contained only one scene throughout its entire length, which was specifically shot by the director, a scene that shows the mass spinning of the Charkha. *Mahatma Gandhi: Twentieth Century Prophet*, was first screened in 1940, the same year that it was completed, at Chennai's Roxy Theatre after due permissions were granted by the Censor Board. The film originally had voiceovers in Tamil, but was later dubbed into Telugu and subsequently into Hindi. The documentary was screened again on the day of India's Independence, 15 August 1947, in New Delhi, where the country's first president Rajendra Prasad arrived to attend the screening. 'Former Prime Minister Indira Gandhi too attended the screening, as her father and then Prime Minister Nehru could not make it to the event', said A. Annamalai, Director of the Gandhi Memorial in an interview given in 2016 to the Hindu.[1]

The documentary was released by Chettiar in the USA in 1953 and subsequently went missing as his efforts to render it in 16mm did not help the film circumvent the technical glitches that plagued it. The new equipment could not support the showing of the film and it sank into oblivion. It surfaced years later in a library in San Francisco, and an abridged version was released for viewing in 2006.[2] It is only thanks to this documentary that the world has access to so many live photos and videos of the great man today.

Gandhi was essayed ten times on-screen by different actors but it would have not been possible to critically analyse each of these films within the span of this research paper. Thus, five of these fictional and quasi-documentary films have been chosen here to demonstrate our findings about films on Gandhi. From amongst these films, only one dealt directly with the life of Mahatma Gandhi, and that was, *Gandhi* (1982) by Richard Attenborough.

Richard Attenborough's Gandhi

Attenborough's film comes closest to being a comprehensive dramatisation of Gandhi's life. It depicts his personal journey through a most significant period of his life; beginning from when he was a twenty-three-year-old barrister freshly out of a London law school in 1893, who found himself at a station in South Africa, having been unceremoniously evicted from the first-class coach in which he had dared to book a seat alongside white men, and ending with his shocking assassination in India in 1948.

The film took twenty years of conceptualisation and

preparation before it was finally made in 1982. Motilal Kothari, an Indian Civil Servant who had been very close to Gandhi, first approached Attenborough to make the film in 1962, and Attenborough convinced himself to agree after reading Louis Fischer's 1951 biography of Gandhi, *Mahatma Gandhi – His Life and Times*.[3] Both Attenborough, who won Best Director at the Oscars in 1983, and Ben Kingsley who won Best Actor at the same ceremony, acknowledged their debt to Motilal Kothari in their acceptance speeches.[4]

Ben Kingsley's interpretation of the Mahatma must go down in history as one of the most perfectly essayed roles in cinema. Throughout the film, one forgets that this is a character being portrayed by an actor because the movie looks so real–Kingsley's shy smile and that mischievous glint in his eyes brings an endearing image of Gandhi to life. From the most intimate and poignant scenes to the incredible crowd scenes, everything is beautifully captured most painstakingly by cinematographers Billy Williams and Ronnie Taylor, with the divine accompanying music flowing from Pandit Ravishankar's sitar. One finds that some of the most breathtaking scenes are shot in rustic settings that are almost bare in their simplicity; women drawing water from a well while Gandhi and his political associates are launching an important campaign; Gandhi throwing his shawl towards a village woman washing clothes in the river, so that she can cover herself, while in the background, the train has ground to a halt atop a bridge as the steam engine hauled trains were wont to do those days–everything feels authentic.

The film tries to be true to the spirit of Gandhi. Gandhi

was a national hero; a stubborn lionheart. Each Indian cherishes his or her own perception and knowledge of Gandhi's role in steering the freedom struggle. However, there were uncomfortable secrets hidden in his personal history that people wished to ignore or gloss over. In the title credits, there is a preamble to the film in which Richard Attenborough writes,

> No man's life can be encompassed in one telling. There is no way to give each year its allotted weight, to include each event, each person who helped to shape a lifetime. What can be done is to be faithful in spirit to the record and try to find one's way to the heart of the man…

The film could not have accommodated the many aspects of Gandhi's life that are missing from the narrative. For instance, MK Gandhi came to be known as a man of truth and non-violence, but at a young age, he had a hard time dealing with these principles and integrating them into his life. According to his autobiography, *My Experiments with Truth*, he was inspired by the *panchsheel* philosophy of Jainism (the five principles that must regulate personal life) and all of his adult life was spent trying to imbibe these values:

- Non-violence – *Ahimsa*
- Truth – *Satya*
- Non-stealing – *Asteya*
- Celibacy/chastity – *Brahmacharya*
- Non-attachment/non-possession – *Aparigraha*

There were several instances in his childhood when

he struggled with insecurities and human follies, having erred and learned from his mistakes. In his childhood, he smoked, stole money, and even ate chicken. One of the most memorable incidents in his life was when he stole a gold chain to clear a debt of twenty-five rupees. Afterwards, he felt extremely guilty about his actions and he confessed to his father, who wept after hearing the young boy out. Gandhi cried too and that became a life-awakening moment for Mohandas Karamchand Gandhi. From then on, he tried to remain steadfast in the path of integrity and truth. This, of course, does not find mention in the film, which begins with Gandhi's life as a young barrister in South Africa.

Again, Gandhi's mother Putli Bai played an important role in his life. She was a great devotee of God and spent much time in prayer. Yet she was knowledgeable about the goings on in her surroundings and commanded respect from people who sought her advice on their problems. Gandhi was influenced by his mother and inspired by her discipline and devotion. In the later years of his life, he is seen to have become very particular about this spiritual aspect of his being. He became strict about his prayer timings, which were fixed. This shows that daily prayers had great significance in his life during the time of his participation in the freedom struggle.

These important aspects of Gandhi's personal life have been omitted from movies that have been made about him; which is unfortunate as these films revolve around Gandhi, and it is essential to look at all the factors responsible for making him what he became, including his philosophy and conduct, whether in the realm of politics, religion, or social life.

Of the *panchsheel* principles, Richard Attenborough's Gandhi touches upon *brahmacharya* (the vow of celibacy) and *aparigraha* (the vow of poverty) through asceticism (refraining from indulgence).

The movie, released on 30 November 1982 and declared tax-free in Bombay (Mumbai) and Delhi, was a high grosser, earning more than 100 crores (Rs 1,000,000,000) in India. In 2010, the Independent Film and Television Alliance (IFTA), a global association representing companies which finance, produce, and license independent films and television programs across countries, selected *Gandhi* as one of the thirty most significant independent films in the last thirty years.

Attenborough says that Pandit Nehru had requested him to make a film on Gandhi, the man with all his frailties and faults, and not to deify him, for Gandhi was no God.

Celibacy/*brahmacharya* was one of the most important practices of his life. Gandhi adopted *brahmacharya* because he believed in strengthening his inner self and eliminating carnal attachment. He was thirteen when he married Kasturba, who was a year older than him, and he had four children with her before taking a vow in 1906, when he had reached his late thirties, to remain celibate for the rest of his life.

Gandhi wrote about this vow in his autobiography He describes how, once, when he was sixteen and tending to his ailing father, and his uncle had come to relieve him at his father's bedside, he had rushed back to his room to have sex with his wife. Soon after, a servant came to inform him that his father was no more. Gandhi said, 'This shame of my carnal desire even at the critical hour of my father's death...is a blot I have never been able to efface or forget...It took me long to get free from the shackles of lust, and I had to pass through many ordeals before I could overcome it'.[5]

In one scene of the film, Mohandas and Kasturba are shown by the banks of the Sabarmati at Porbandar, relating with nostalgia the details of their marriage ceremony to an American reporter Vince Walker (a fictional character inspired by American journalist Webb Miler). Ba and Bapu enact the scene of their marriage ceremony, circling an imaginary holy fire while they take their vows. The manner and words of Kasturba's recitation presage Gandhi's eventual withdrawal from the carnal pleasures of marriage.[6]

Gandhi's preaching and practice of chastity involved many strange experiments but not much is written about these in available texts and documents. In our research, we found some major evidence in the National Archives of India, Delhi, in the form of his personal letters and the interviews he gave to journalists, researchers, and social activists. There were also the letters and diaries written by Manu (Mridula Gandhi), his grandniece and an ardent admirer, who talks about the celibacy experiments in the ashram. Manu's diary was in Gujrati, her mother tongue, but it was later translated into Hindi and English. The diary entries reveal the extent to which she and others were psychologically affected by Gandhi's experiments with his sexuality, of which they were a part. For instance, on 28 December 1946, she writes in her diary from Srirampur, Bihar, 'Bapu is a mother to me. He is initiating me to a higher human plane through the *Brahmacharya* experiments, part of his Mahayagna of character-building. Any loose talk about the experiment is most condemnable.'[7]

Film actress Supriya Pathak plays Manuben in the movie, but all suggestions of Gandhi's sexual experiments are carefully removed from her portrayal, one might say in an attempt to elevate Gandhi the man to the sublime stature of Gandhi the Mahatma.

His views on communal amity between the Hindus and Muslims are depicted in several scenes of the film making it evident how important that aspect of Gandhi's value system is to the director, Richard Attenborough. In one scene Gandhi talks wistfully of his childhood with Walker (Martin Sheen). He says he was raised Hindu, but the priest at his temple would also read from the Quran. This left a strong impression on Gandhi; at one point he tells his followers, 'I am a Muslim and a Hindu and a Christian and a Jew and so are all of you'.

The sequence of his visit to Noakhali in Calcutta at the peak of the communal riots post-partition showing Gandhi's desperate plea for communal harmony, for which he is willing to fast until death, is shot by the director with missionary zeal.

In addition, there are scenes in the movie that depict other aspects of Gandhi's beliefs and personal character. His opposition to the caste system and his determination to abolish untouchability is shown in an incident in which Gandhi gets violent with Kasturba when she refuses to clean the toilets, saying that it is the work of an untouchable. The fact that he gets furious with Kasturba and apologises to her later shows that while he is fighting against injustices in society, he is also fighting his personal battles. His vegetarianism—where he is feeding and tending to the goat whose milk, he loves to drink; his preference for swadeshi–he is shown in his later years spinning the charkha incessantly and only wearing a homespun *dhoti* and *chadar*; and his mischievousness–before he launches his salt satyagraha, when Vince Walker asks him, 'Now, wait a minute. You know what you are going to do, don't you?' Gandhi replies with twinkling eyes, 'It would have been very uncivil of me to let you make such a long trip for nothing'; all these incidents are cleverly woven into the film, showing us how MK Gandhi adapted his personal beliefs and idiosyncrasies into his ideologies, which he then used to strategie the freedom struggle.

Gandhi as the Indigenous Political Solution

Gandhi said 'The politician in me has never dominated a single decision of mine, and if I seem to take part in politics, it is only because politics encircle us today like the coil of a snake from which one cannot get out, no matter how much one tries. I wish, therefore, to wrestle with the snake'.[8]

Gandhi assumed the leadership of the Indian National Congress in 1922. The first responsibility he took on himself as president was to expand the reach of the party among the masses living in the remotest corners of the country. Believing rural India to be the backbone of the country, Gandhi travelled extensively to India's villages, far and near, crisscrossing the country by train, bullock cart, or on foot. These visits are beautifully captured in Attenborough's *Gandhi*. The fact that he had embraced poverty is borne out by his travelling cattle class quite literally. In one scene, he is sitting amidst villagers and their domestic animals, and is seen alighting from a third-class compartment while at the same time, Sardar Patel alights from a First-class coach, with a wry smile on his face.

Richard Attenborough's *Gandhi* shows Gandhi's growth as a social activist and reformer before he jumped into the political fray on his return to India. Dealing in a detailed manner with the first Satyagraha and non-cooperation movements he led in South Africa, the film goes on to show how Gandhi experimented successfully with the same revolutionary strategy against the Indigo merchants in Champaran. Similarly, the incident at Chauri Chaura, in the Gorakhpur district of the United Province presently known as Uttar Pradesh, in which more than twenty policemen are locked into a police station which is then set on fire by angry revolutionaries taking part in the non-cooperation movement initiated by Gandhi in 1922, and its impact on Gandhi is shown to chilling effect in the film! Gandhi called off the movement and proceeded on a six-day fast to show his agony at what had happened.

The civil disobedience movement forced the British to call Gandhi to the second round-table conference in 1931, though unfortunately, it did not produce the outcome everyone in India was hoping for—the discussion of the modalities for her independence. During this visit, Gandhi's last to England, he is seen visiting with the workers of the Lancashire cotton mills who appear to adore him.

Indeed, there are many scenes in which we are shown Gandhi's popularity amongst the foreign press and the goodwill he enjoyed with the common white population. The sequence in which Margaret Bourke White (played by Candice Bergen), an American journalist from Life Magazine, comes to photograph Gandhi, brings out his extremely charming personality.

The film also covers his many fasts, some of which were to promote non-violent means of protest and some for communal harmony. The cost to Gandhi's health is evident as the man grows increasingly frail even as his stature as a statesman grows to monumental proportions. This is depicted especially well in the scene showing the 5-day fast unto death that he undertook in Kolkata, which witnessed horrendous Hindu-Muslim riots in August and September of 1947, after the declaration of Independence.

Attenborough integrates Gandhi's frequent stints in jail into the film to show that Gandhi's political strategy required breaking unjust laws but also accepting the consequences of his actions and going to prison for them.

His political leadership was mainly based on morality and religiosity, advocating the tenets of *ahimsa* and *satyagraha* which were the basis of all religions. In one sequence, he is seen telling his friend and admirer Charlie Andrews about how the New Testament, too, talks about non-violence. He asks Charles Andrew to stop visiting him as he wishes his fellow countrymen to see him as being squarely on their side but his position is clear on what he sees as *sarva dharma sama bhava*, a unity of all religions.

Though his shrewd political activism is emphasised, he is also shown as a social reformer who campaigned tirelessly for communal harmony and the abolition of unfortunate practices such as untouchability. The scenes depicting Gandhi asking his wife to clean the toilets, or asking Maulana Azad to give him his glass of juice are explicitly meant to display this side of his persona.

We must understand that Gandhi was a pragmatist. He was not any democratically elected leader and he had his own style of leadership that was not always based on sound principles of democracy and politics. He understood that it is not humanly possible to always balance and create harmony between varied moralities and we have to settle at times for the lesser of two evils, an option that would cause lesser damage, because at times, causing damage is inevitable. Thus, when the idea of partition is proposed and Jinnah gives Gandhi the option to choose between a civil war and two nations, Gandhi chooses to take Nehru and Patel's side, which he believed to be the side with the lesser evil.

Depiction of Gandhi in Other Films

Gandhi emerges in his political avatar rather more clearly in Jabbar Patel's 2002 biopic, *Dr Babasaheb Ambedkar: The Untold Truth* than in Attenborough's film, though Patel's film is not about Gandhi per se. A young Gandhi, played by the late Mohan Gokhale, is seen here not as a saintly figure but as a political strategist who takes a confrontationist stance with Ambedkar. The deep ideological differences between Gandhi and Dr Bhimrao Ambedkar on the question of the caste system are brought out in the film through the two leaders' first meeting at Mani Bhavan in Bombay, and later at the Round

Table Conference meeting where they spar over who is to be taken as the true representative of the untouchables, and at Aga Khan Palace, during the deliberations on the Poona Pact.

In this film, Gandhi is portrayed as Dr Ambedkar sees him, a Hindu religious leader who is keen to protect Hinduism but does not give much importance to the emancipation of the depressed classes. Ambedkar is shown as being at the end of his patience with the discriminatory and unjust system of caste, which he wishes to have abolished, while Gandhi is seen arguing for its reform. Gandhi never abandoned the Varna Ashram Dharma and its classifications which underlie the caste system, and one sees in Ambedkar an utterly disillusioned man fighting with Gandhi from a self-proclaimed position as the sole representative and voice of the lower castes. Gandhi however holds Ambedkar in high esteem. In one scene, Gandhi is shown asking Nehru to appoint Ambedkar as the Law Minister of independent India because he feels that when one who has suffered at the hands of the system writes the laws of the country, only then can every citizen, no matter what background they came from, expect to get justice.

Rajkumar Santoshi's, *The Legend of Bhagat Singh*, which was released in 2002, shows Gandhi in an unflattering light. It is clear that the heart of the film lies with the militant freedom fighters, Bhagat Singh, Rajguru, and Sukhdev, and their opposition to the Congress party's policies and decisions under Gandhi's guidance. The latter was overtly critical of the revolutionaries and their methods (shown clearly in the scene where the congress leaders express their strong condemnation of the parliament bombing as having brought shame to the freedom movement). In return,

Bhagat Singh (played by Ajay Devgan) is shown publicly ridiculing Gandhi's moves. There is a scene in which Bhagat Singh forcefully rejects Gandhi's acceptance of Dominion Status for India in 1928, arguing that the move would simply bring the upper-class Indians to rule over the average Indian. In another scene, Gandhi (played by Surendra Rajan) is seen receiving a bouquet of black roses from the protesters who accuse him of having let down the revolutionaries. The lame expression with which Gandhi accepts the bouquet lowers him in the eyes of the audience.

The film is an unabashed eulogisation of Bhagat Singh at the expense of Gandhi. It debunks many of the ideals Gandhi stood for including his faith in religion (Bhagat Singh takes pride in being an atheist) and his advocacy of *ahimsa*, which Bhagat Singh and his associates believe is absolutely ineffectual as a strategy to engage with the might of the British Empire.

Bhagat Singh rose to popularity after his 114-day hunger strike with his associates in jail, against the inhuman treatment of prisoners. Initially, he followed Gandhi and adopted his methods of Satyagraha. But when Gandhi withdrew from the Non-cooperation movement after the Chauri Chaura incident, Bhagat Singh broke away from him and turned towards Marxism and thereafter became a radical communist. The movie shows Bhagat Singh having a huge following among the young members of the Congress and even Nehru is seen appreciating him which poses a threat to Gandhi's popularity amongst the youth, especially the Naujawan Bharat Sabha.

Interestingly even though Nehru has been credited

with the declaration/demand for 'Poorna Swaraj' (total independence instead of Dominion status), it was another Congress leader, the famous poet Hasrat Mohani, who was the first activist to demand Poorna Swaraj from the British at the 1921 Ahmedabad session of the Indian National Congress. Hasrat Mohani also coined the term 'Inquilab Zindabaad' in 1921, which was popularised by Bhagat Singh and his comrades who had fervently backed Nehru in his call for Poorna Swaraj. The slogan 'Inquilab Zindabad' caught the public imagination and started replacing 'Vande Mataram', which had been favoured by Gandhi.

The film also propagates the perception amongst a large segment of India's population that Gandhi did not make a strong enough effort to stop the hanging of the three revolutionaries. Gandhi is shown attending a meeting with Lord Irwin and asking him to at least delay the hanging, but Irwin denies the request and Gandhi leaves it at that. Historically, no meeting took place, it was only an exchange of letters between Irwin and Gandhi. There is a scene where he tells the protesters who confront him on the matter that he could not have sided with violence or with anyone using violent means. In this and other scenes, Gandhi comes across as weak and wavering.

Surendra Ranjan plays a very brief cameo as Gandhi in Shyam Benegal's biopic, *Netaji Subhas Chandra Bose: The Forgotten Hero* (2004), appearing right at the beginning of the film, even before the credits, as the director sets the background to Bose's political journey. The scene depicts the ideological conflict between Gandhi and Bose but at the same shows Gandhi adopting an indulgent and fatherly attitude towards Bose, calling him a '*bigda hua beta*' and saying that their goal is the same but their paths are different. However, he does not mince words in showing Bose how their paths are indeed diametrically opposite. Gandhi is not willing to accept violence in any form and Subhash Chandra Bose insists on snatching the right to total self-governance from the British by force. Gandhi tells Bose that he will not under any circumstance adopt violent means and the latter must either forsake violence and follow the path of non-violence against the British or quit as President of the Congress. He and Nehru look on regretfully as Bose's action signals that he has chosen to quit. The film is about Subhash Chandra Bose and Gandhi simply provides the initial starting point to his activities as he escapes abroad and attempts to steer the INA by remote control, so to speak. Yet in the mind of the audience, it clearly fixes an image of Gandhi as a shrewd political strategist and a stubborn propagator of his own beliefs.

This does not do justice to Gandhi, who we must understand was an ardent supporter of *ahimsa* or non-violence, and wanted more than anything to appeal to the conscience of the oppressor so as to make them understand what they were doing was wrong and that an eye for an eye would make the whole world blind. We, as human beings, have learnt that revenge has its own vicious circle.

Depiction of Gandhi's Philosophy in Movies

Certainly, movies play a crucial role in the understanding of our daily life. Biopics, sci-fi, romcoms, action, suspense, mystery, and crime thrillers all help open our eyes to the ideas and values that make us who we are. A film may get appreciation, criticism, or mixed reviews for many reasons, but to our astonishment, we find that there is no prize anywhere for the true characterisation of historical figures. The films that have been considered so far tried to remain faithful while portraying 'Gandhi the person'—a shrewd politician, a strict disciplinarian, a man of morals and of religion—the man who became Mahatma. However, in today's world, Gandhi is more an idea than a historical person. His name has become synonymous with the philosophy of peace and non-violence, having the potency to transform the thoughts and actions of people and nations. The success or failure of a film on Gandhi must also be judged on whether or not it has succeeded in conveying his philosophical message to the audience. And interestingly, it emerges that, compared to the other films, there is only one that has achieved incredible success in popularising Gandhi's philosophy, and that is Richard Attenborough's film, *Gandhi*.

From the beginning, it becomes evident that more than anything, the director of the film is keen to depict Gandhi as a prophet of peace and non-violence.

Ahimsa and *satyagraha* encompass the entire span of Gandhi's philosophy. *Ahimsa*, quite simply rendered as non-violence, permeated everything he said and did. He practised non-violence in thought, word, and deed, and Gandhi incorporated nonviolence into his social and political action as much as into his daily routine. He wrote extensively about it in his many publications. In one newspaper, Gandhi writes 'Non-violence is a power which can be wielded equally by all–children, young men and women or grown-up people, provided they have a living faith in the God of Love and have therefore equal love for all mankind. When non-violence is accepted as the law of life, it must pervade the whole being and not be applied to isolated acts'.[9] In another, he writes, 'My non-violence does not admit of running away from danger and leaving dear ones unprotected. Between violence and cowardly flight, I can only prefer violence to cowardice. I can no more preach non-violence to a coward than I can tempt a blind man to enjoy healthy scenes'.[10]

For Gandhi, *ahimsa* went hand in hand with Satyagraha, formed out of two words, '*satya*' or truth (itself formed out of the Sanskrit root '*sat*' meaning 'that which has being') and '*agraha*' meaning 'to seize firmly'. *Satyagraha* literally means 'remaining firmly devoted to truth'. Gandhi used *satyagraha* primarily as a political strategy aimed at winning over an adversary without taking recourse to violence.

Gandhi explained to his followers what was meant by satyagraha in practice.

> A '*satyagrahi*', is a civil resister; one who harbours no anger at his opponents but suffers with humility their anger; bears their assaults without retaliating or submitting out of fear of punishment to any order given in anger. Non-retaliation includes no swearing and cursing or insulting one's opponent with unsavoury words.

Indeed, Gandhi went on to add,

> In the course of the struggle, if anyone insults an official or commits an assault upon him, a civil resister will protect

such official or officials from the insult or attack even at the risk of his own life.[11]

Beginning with the scenes of civil disobedience in South Africa where Gandhi is seen thrusting the identity passes issued specifically to Asians, into the fire even while the police thrash him repeatedly, to the contrived scenes of the Salt Satyagraha at Dandi, Gujrat, where hundreds of Indian men and women are seen marching forward to make salt, arms resolutely by their sides, only to be mercilessly struck down by the blows of the British police, the emphasis in Attenborough's film is on Gandhi's ideal of Ahimsa not only as a philosophy but as a unique political weapon against the oppressor.[12] Gandhi is frequently seen meeting with people whether his own countrymen or the British officials and other foreign visitors with his palms always closed in a gesture of gentle supplication, though his steel-like courage is visible to all. The depiction of his fasts against communal violence, the withdrawal of the non-cooperation movement after the Chauri Chaura violence, his willingness to court arrest rather than use force even in self-defence, all have the same purpose.

In *Dr Babasaheb Ambedkar* (2000), *The Legend of Bhagat Singh* (2002), and *Netaji Subhash Chandra Bose: The Forgotten Hero* (2004), where Gandhi has a minuscule presence, he is presented through someone else's vision—Babasaheb Ambedkar, Bhagat Singh and his fellow revolutionaries and sympathisers, and Subhash Chandra Bose respectively. They were serious semi-biographical films trying to do justice to the towering personalities from Indian history, and even though Gandhi's character was not central to these films, important aspects of it, for instance, his steadfastness towards nonviolence and his unwavering faith in *satyagraha* were given prominence in all of them. Yet the spirit of Gandhi is missing from these films. Instead, it took a completely fictional, light-hearted comedy like Raj Kumar Hirani and Vidhu Vinod Chopra's *Lage Raho Munna Bhai* (2006), to carry the true spirit of Gandhi's message and his philosophy to the remotest corners of the country. *Lage Raho Munna Bhai* touched the minds and hearts of the people with its ingenuous message of 'love everyone, even your enemy', like no other film that came before it. By calling it *Gandhigiri*, the film made Gandhi's philosophy eminently accessible to the masses. To them, it meant winning your opponent over with gestures of love and peace offerings instead of threats and terror tactics.

This message permeated all the subplots of the film as well; when Munna encourages Victor the taxi driver to tell the truth to his father that he has squandered away the latter's hard earned money; when, inspired by Munna and Jahnvi's talk show, a retired clerk disrobes in front of a corrupt government official in an apparent bid to pay him with articles of his personal attire, for the release of his pension papers; when under Gandhi's exhortation, Munna himself confesses to his lady love that he is no history professor; when the pandit shows his cowardly fear of death even though he has been posing as an accomplished religious guru with powers to foresee the future; when the groom (played by Abhishek Bachchan) goes ahead and marries Lucky Singh's daughter even though the Guru has warned him that he would die early if he married this particular girl; every story woven into the main theme is fragrant with some or other Gandhian value, be it peace, truth, nonviolence, reason over blind prejudice, or love and compassion.

A good part of the credit for the success of *Lage Raho* goes to Dilip Prabhavalkar for his endearing and convincing portrayal of Gandhi as a ghost guiding, exhorting, and inspiring the lovable *tapori* Sanjay Dutt and his sidekick, 'Circuit', to carry on the crusade against the wily and unscrupulous building contractor, Lucky Singh (Boman Irani) to force him to return the house, which is home to a group of elderly people living by themselves. Munna tells people how to apply the principles of truth and ahimsa, Gandhi's ultimate tools for social change, in practical everyday situations. With the right amount of humor and sarcasm, and a presentation of real issues that concern today's society, the film achieved remarkable commercial success.

Some Other Points of Comparison

Why do we watch films? How does the maker ensure a desired response from a diverse audience? What is it about a film that affects the way we think about things?

A filmmaker employs many tools to make a film tell a convincing story or at least establish its credentials as good cinema. A fictional story comes alive on screen and manages to hold its audience captive when all elements of the film, plot, dialogues, setting, characters, sound, and light, come together to deliver a believable tale with which the audience can engage at a personal level. Similarly, a piece of history is authentically recreated on screen when actors enact the best possible portrayal of characters, suitable locations are chosen with attention to the story, music and sound are integrated into the storyline seamlessly and costumes and background scenery create the correct ambience. Every element is important and the slightest mismatch between any of them can affect the convincing power of a film and its impact on the audience.

Can you imagine anyone attired in flamboyant clothes playing Gandhi the revolutionary Mahatma in a film? Surely not for that would be incongruous. Attention to costume design is a primary concern of filmmakers. Indeed, Gandhi himself allegedly chose to appear in a simple 'dhoti' and 'chadar' so that he could identify with India's village folk, the poor and the backwards, who could not have accepted him into their midst had he worn clothes different from them.

Similarly, for an accurate portrayal of a character, whether fictional or historical, an actor must get the right inflexion of voice, personal mannerisms, gait, and other behavioural idiosyncrasies of the real or imagined persona.

The intention of the maker also affects the way films fare. The interpersonal relations among different characters of the film must be developed carefully for the film to tell the story as the director intends it to be told. The quality of a film will suffer if sufficient screen time and space is not given to each character, the lead cast as well as those playing bit roles.

On comparing the portrayal of Gandhi in the five movies chosen for this project, one can easily trace how the characterisations differ in accordance with the intention to show Gandhi in a particular light. Richard Attenborough's Gandhi was the obvious protagonist around which the story revolved, and the director intended to elevate Gandhi to the status of a Mahatma. He presented Gandhi as a heroic figure, doing everything possible to create a larger-than-life image on screen.

In hindsight, one can say perhaps that no other actor could have played Gandhi so convincingly as Ben Kingsley did. He did a superlative job in the role and it might have helped that he had a Gujarati father and his name was actually Krishna Pandit Bhanji. At the same time, it is imperative to give equal credit to the film's excellent supporting cast.

Along with finely nuanced characterisations, Attenborough planned every other element carefully to make this a remarkable film. *Gandhi* was acknowledged worldwide as a piece of great cinema because of the extensive research and extreme attention to finer details that went into its making. Theatre director Amal Allana, who worked in the art department and was a set dresser in the film, talks about the enormous amount of digging into all sorts of research material the team had to do. 'One had to pore over historical, architectural, photographic, and design sources, as well as rely on the evidence of living witnesses', she said. All of this must have taken several days and hours.

According to the Guinness Book of World Records, Attenborough used the maximum ever number of extras, (over three lakhs), to create Gandhi's funeral scene alone. Not just that, he arranged food and water for everyone for the duration of the shooting of the scene.[13]

The cinematography added depth to the characters. The movie was shot in Panavision, with a unique new gadget called the 'Louma crane' for the camera to be mounted on. It was an extremely delicate piece of equipment and expensive too–at the time Gandhi was made, only five such cranes existed in the world. As director of photography, Billy Williams later said the unpredictable Indian weather and winds played havoc with the Louma crane and the camera teams were ultimately forced to move back to the more popularly used manual cranes.

Gandhi won eight out of the eleven Oscar nominations it received in different categories, including the Oscar for Best Director, Best Actor, and Best Costume Design.

The biopics, *Bose: The Forgotten Hero, Dr. Bhimrao Ambedkar*, and *The Legend of Bhagat Singh*, despite their many sympathisers, did not come close to Attenborough's film. To be fair, they were not pro-Gandhi films. There was no attempt to glorify Gandhi or to elevate his image. Instead, the films showed him in a rather unflattering light as an ordinary individual, a political leader and strategist whose methods were unconventional, controversial, and of doubtful efficacy. The intention was to provide a counterpoint that would enhance the stature of their respective leads at the expense of downsizing the Mahatma. But with this intention, they did not achieve much success and the films could not manage to leave a significant mark.

Subhash Chandra Bose: The Forgotten Hero suffered due to its duration; it felt too lengthy and this deflected the audience's attention away from the central theme. Oscar-winning documentary filmmaker, Alex Gibney in an interview on BBC says, 'a biopic makes an indelible impact'. Feature filmmakers must have the right approach while doing biopics and not try to pack in too much biographical information. 'I think the ones that are less successful are the ones that dutifully try to do everything, and in trying to do everything, end up with nothing.'[14]

Rajkumar Santoshi's biopic, *The Legend of Bhagat*

Singh, tanked at the Box office but received some good critical reviews, a couple of National Awards, including Best Feature Film in Hindi, and a bunch of jury prizes at the Filmfare awards. The film is witness to the director's wish to do for Bhagat Singh and his fellow revolutionaries, what Attenborough did for Gandhi–establish him as a shining hero; an unforgettable son of India!

Ajay Devgan won the National Award as Best Actor for essaying the eponymous role and bringing fire and intensity to the character. He is ably supported by Sushant Singh as Sukhdev, D. Santos as Rajguru, and Akhilendra Mishra as Chandra Shekhar Azad. The dialogues by Piyush Mishra reflect Bhagat Singh's erudition and wit, and they contributed significantly towards the film's impact. A. R. Rahman's music and Sonu Nigam's vocals added to its aesthetics.

Dr. Babasaheb Ambedkar: The Untold Story, was a sort of official presentation of the government of Maharashtra, along with the Ministry of Social Justice and Empowerment, which funded the film. The fact that it was dubbed in nine languages extended its reach. Many of Ambedkar's dialogues in the film incorporate texts actually written by him. Although Mammootty won the National Award for Best Actor as Ambedkar, and the film won the awards for Best Feature Film in English and Best Art Direction, the film failed to carry much weight commercially.

Gandhi is shown here as cunning, selfish, and always anxious to outwit Dr Ambedkar and get his own way. To preempt criticism from the censor board at such a portrayal of the man who came to be revered as the father of the Nation,

Jabbar Patel, in an interview with Pritish Nandy says, 'After all, you must remember that this was the early Gandhi. He became a saint later. He was much more intolerant, much more difficult during this phase and that is why he made things so difficult for Dr Ambedkar'.[15]

Indian commercial cinema takes its songs and music very seriously. In Bollywood culture specifically, a movie cannot be imagined without songs or a dance number even though it may have nothing to do with the subject of the film or have, at best, a very flimsy connection with the story.

Songs can either blow a fresh breath of air in between scenes breaking the monotony for the viewers or they can totally distract attention from the main storyline. *Lage Raho Munna Bhai* proved to be a sharp contrast to the other four in this regard. It aspired to be a mainstream film and used the song-and-dance routine to get its message across. Yet it did it sensibly and with sensitivity without hampering the film's mainstay, the ideology of *Gandhigiri*. The film conveyed the Gandhian ideals of truth and nonviolence in a manner that appealed to the youth and so managed to connect with its target audience in a way that the other films did not.

The Relevance of Gandhi Films in the Twenty first Century

We are faced with an intriguing situation here. Cinema, through its diversity, creative style, and deep reach, is a universal language through which it is possible to influence millions. Yet, for a complex, multi-faceted personality such as Gandhi who literally spun the threads that bound a diverse population into one nation; whose ideals inspired vast majorities across the world; about whom Einstein thought that future generations would never believe that a man such as he had ever walked the earth; whose life was a symbol of truth and nonviolence, the two pillars on which the Republic of India could stand tall; and most of all, in a country that churns out the highest number of movies in the world, the cinematic output on this man's life and philosophy is astonishingly meagre. It appears that even while the larger world failed to appreciate cinema's potential to take Gandhi to the masses and keep him alive in the hearts and minds of ordinary people, Gandhi too, at the same time, failed to capitalise on a medium of communication that could have helped in mobilising people in large numbers for his several action programs.

It is all the more surprising because Gandhi had a very astute understanding of the power of symbols and how they could be used to convey his message. He used the Charkha, his spinning wheel, to exhort Indians towards sacrificing foreign-made goods and adopting *swadeshi*. He used his simple attire to spread his message of simple and austere living. So why didn't he see the great power of films to shape people's perceptions and mould their responses to suit the national freedom movement? Why didn't he use movies to spread his message into the deep interiors of the country?

The fact is that Gandhi had a loathing for films and thought them to be a product of immoral technology. He thought that it would corrupt the youth. He expressed his distaste in many interviews and writings.

I have never once been to a cinema and refuse to be

enthused about it and waste God-given time in spite of pressure sometimes used by kind friends. They tell me it has an educational value. It is possible that it has. But its corrupting influence obtrudes itself upon me every day. Education, therefore, I seek elsewhere.[16]

And again, in a speech to the menial workers in Burma, he said,
The cinema, the stage, the race course, the drink booth and the opium den—all these enemies of society that have sprung up under the fostering influence of the present system threaten us on all sides.[17]

Gandhi's vision for an Independent India as a self-sufficient country, embedded with the two ideals of truth and non-violence, never became a reality. We have not followed his simple yet powerful message of respecting human dignity, nonviolence, and self-determination, and have ended up building a society in which his ethics and ideals have almost no place. Gandhi never approved of or endorsed a system in which a single party would wield power. He emphasised selfless service to the country. He embodied a willingness to sacrifice self-interest and focused on his concern for others—values which are fast disappearing from the minds of people. Gandhi's political ideology, which emphasised decentralisation of power—village panchayats assuming more control in public affairs, trusteeship of wealth, an indigenous education system, basic sanitation, abolition of the barbaric practices of dowry, untouchability and prohibition of widow remarriage—and other such goals, has lost the relevance it once had.

However, Gandhi has been kept alive to this date as a symbol of peace, and no matter what madness prevails in the world, people can never devalue peace among nations, among communities, and among societies. Of all the films that were considered here, *Lage Raho Munna Bhai* consciously tried to locate Gandhi's values in the contemporary world. It found a resonance in an anxious society ridden by caste, class, ethnic and communal conflicts, with its promise of a Utopian world where the perpetrators of violence and corruption could be magically transformed by the power of love. It achieved an unexpected connection with the audience too.

Attenborough's Gandhi continues to have relevance as a supremely well-made biopic on an extremely important figure in Indian and World history. It is telecast each year when Gandhi's birth anniversary is celebrated on 2 October or his death anniversary is observed on 30 January, though its audience mostly comprises members of the older generation.

The Legend of Bhagat Singh and the other films do not hold any appeal for the youth of today in a general sense, even though some young people may see glimpses of themselves in a Bhagat Singh or a Bose. In any case, not all aspects of Gandhi's life could have been encapsulated in a single film, and the said films neither claimed to nor tried to, present a comprehensive portrayal of Gandhi which could be used as a pocket edition of what Gandhi stood for.

ENDNOTES

INTRODUCTION

1. Bazin, A (1971) *What is cinema*. Translated by Hugh Gray, University of California Press, Vol. 2, pp. 26; Retrieved from https://fadingtheaesthetic.files.wordpress.com/2013/03/bazin-andre-what-is-cinema-volume-2-kg.pdf
2. Stanford Encyclopedia of Philosophy (2004) *Philosophy of film*, 1. The Idea of a Philosophy of Film [Online] Retrieved from https://plato.stanford.edu/entries/film/
3. Stanford Encyclopedia of Philosophy (2004) *Philosophy of film*, 1. The Idea of a Philosophy of Film [Online] Retrieved from https://plato.stanford.edu/entries/film/

A GUIDE TO PHILOSOPHISING CINEMA BY PROFESSOR V. SANIL

1. Wolters, Eugene (2013) *Alain Badiou is making a movie about Plato with Brad Pitt and Sean Connery* [Online] Critical Theory. Retrieved from http://www.critical-theory.com/alain-badiou-writing-script-movie-plato-brad-pitt-sean-connery/ [Accessed 13 August 2020].
2. University of Washington (2015) *The allegory of the cave* [Online] Retrieved from https://faculty.washington.edu/smcohen/320/cave.htm [Accessed 13 August 2020].

3   Noel, Carroll (1998) *A philosophy of mass art.* Oxford: Oxford University Press.
4   Giles Deleuze's *Cinema 1: The Movement-Image and Cinema 2: The Time-Image* (translated into English in 1986 and 1989 respectively). His 'Cinema books' as they are called, are well-known, if problematic, texts on film studies.
5   Event theory sees a film as an event or made up of segments or units which may be a single scene or cluster of scenes called 'events'.
6   Bordwell, David (1996) 'Contemporary film studies and the vicissitudes of grand theory'. In:David Bordwell & Noel Carroll, (eds) (1996) pp.19. Madison: University of Wisconsin Press, Wisconsin. P.19. *Post Theory: Reconstructing Film Studies.*
7   Cavell, Stanley (1981) *Pursuits of happiness: the hollywood comedy of remarriage.* Cambridge Mass; Harvard University Press.
8   Mulhall, Stephen (2002) *On film: thinking in action.* Routledge; London & New York. He also considers many other films for instance in the list of films doing philosophy, including the 1999 hit The Matrix, Memento (2000), and Eternal Sunshine of the Spotless Mind (2004).
9   A guided design model in teaching-learning aims to enhance a student's decision-making skills, by throwing at them prompts, questions, cues, and quizzes, even while imparting conceptual knowledge and principles.
10 Stanford Encyclopedia of Philosophy (2004) *Philosophy of film,* 7. Film as Philosophy [Online] Retrieved from https://plato.stanford.edu/entries/film/#FilSouKnoAndIns [Accessed

11 August 2020].

11 The manifesto initially imitated the wording of François Truffaut's 1954 essay in Cahiers du Cinema, *Une certaine tendance du cinéma français*. It was released at a gathering in Paris (March 1995) of filmmakers and associated film personalities who had met to celebrate the first century of motion pictures and to discuss the uncertain future facing commercial cinema. Called upon to speak about the future of film, Lars von Trier astonished the audience by distributing the red pamphlets that announced his 'manifesto'. Wikipedia. Dogme 95. Retrieved from https://en.wikipedia. org/wiki/Dogme_95

12 Wikipedia. *Dogme 95*. Retrieved from https://en.wikipedia.org/wiki/Dogme_95 [Accessed 16 December 2020].

13 Sanil, V (2004) *Passing time: Immanuel Kant goes to the cinema*. '200 Years of Kant', an Indian Philosophical Quarterly Special Number, edited by Sharad Deshpande, Vol. 31, Nos. 1-4, pp. 253. Retrieved from https://www.academia.edu/29274541/Philosophy_and_Hindi_Cinema;%20%20accessed%20on%20 14-12-2020 [Accessed 14 December 2020].

FILM AND CULTURE: INVITING NEW VOICES AND NEWER VISIONS

1 Lustig, Myron; Koester, Jolene (2010) *Intercultural competence: Interpersonal communication across cultures.* 6th Edn. Allyn & Bacon, Pearson.P.46.

2 Vebhuti Duggal's presentation in the symposium was entitled, *Ubiquitous listening: radios, public space, and film sound in north India,* c. 1952-1975

3   Mahiema is referring here to the previous presentation made by an independent filmmaker and cinema academic, Sudipto Sen.
4   'Filmed entirely in India, this transmedia project was developed with support from artists, volunteers, hackers, and friends in New Delhi, India; Ryerson and York Universities, Canada; Code for Boston, USA; and the Open Documentary Lab at MIT, USA.' Retrieved from http://www.aashiyaan.org/en/ [Accessed 14 March 2021].

THE RESURGENCE OF FILM: THE ARRIVAL OF PARALLEL CINEMA AND THE NEW WAVE

1   'Mise en scène, pronounced meez-ahn-sen, is a term used to describe the setting of a scene in a play or a film. It refers to everything placed on the stage or in front of the camera– including people. In other words, mise en scène is a catch-all for everything that contributes to the visual presentation and overall "look" of a production. When translated from French, it means "placing on stage"'. MasterClass (2021) *What is mise en scène in film?* Retrieved from https://www.masterclass.com/articles/what-is-mise-en-scene-in-film [Accessed on 22 October 2022].
2   In 1948, Alexandre Astruc published *The birth of the new avant-garde: the camera-stylo,* a manifesto outlining the power of cinema as an artistic tool. He argued that cinema could rival the creative possibilities of literature and traditional artwork, and therefore showed disdain towards the commercialisation of the relatively new medium. These values were passionately shared by the critics of Cahiers

du cinema who collectively continued to explore Astruc's principles and develop their vision, which would become known as auteur theory (La politique des auteurs).
3   Parallel Cinema quite literally meant an alternative to mainstream commercial cinema. Parallel Cinema was also called art cinema. The movement originated in the late 1940s in Bengal with the works of Satyajit Ray, Ritwik Ghatak, and Mrinal Sen, but soon branched out into the rest of India. Tapan Sen, Khwaja Ahmad Abbas, Shyam Benegal, Adoor Gopalakrishnan, Girish Karnad, and Buddhadeb Dasgupta made films that were remarkable for their aesthetics and innovative style. The movement also included the films of the more commercially successful film directors such as Bimal Rai, Chetan Anand, Guru Dutt, and V. Shantaram.
4   Bhaskar, Ira (2013) The Indian new wave.In:Gokulsing et. al.(eds)(2013) *Routledge handbook of Indian cinemasLondon: Routledge*. Retrieved from https://www.routledgehandbooks.com/doi/10.4324/9780203556054.ch3

CINEMATIC REFLECTIONS ON REALITY: REALISM AND NEOREALISM

1   Braudy, Leo; Cohen, Marshall (eds.) (1999) *Film theory and criticism*. Oxford: Oxford University Press.
2   The Centro Sperimentale di Cinematographia, alternatively the Experimental Film Centre or Italian National Film School, is the oldest film school in Western Europe. It was established, in 1935 in Rome, Italy, by Benito Mussolini's head of cinema, Luigi Freddi. It aimed to promote cinema and the art and craft of cinematography throughout Italy.

The centre, founded in Rome in 1935, was and still is financed by the Italian government and focuses on education, research, publication, and theory. About the Italian National Film School [Online] Promovendux. Retrieved from https://promovendux.com/universities/italian-national-film-school/

3   Deep focus is a style or technique of cinematography and staging with great depth of field, using relatively wide-angle lenses and small lens apertures to render in sharp focus near and distant planes simultaneously. A deep-focus shot includes foreground, middle-ground, and extreme-background objects, all in focus – The Columbia Film Language Glossary, *Deep Focus*. Retrieved from https://filmglossary.ccnmtl.columbia.edu/term/deep-focus/.

4   In Diegesis the story is recounted by the narrator, as opposed to being shown or enacted. Details about the world itself and the experiences of its characters are revealed explicitly through the narrative. The narrator presents the actions (and sometimes thoughts) of the characters to the readers or audience. Diegetic elements are part of the fictional world (part of the story), as opposed to non-diegetic elements which are stylistic elements of how the narrator tells the story (part of the storytelling). *Diegesis*. Retrieved from https://en.wikipedia.org/wiki/Diegesis [Accessed 31 December 2020].

5   *Poetic Realism*. Retrieved from https://en.wikipedia.org/wiki/Poetic_realism [Accessed 30 December 2020].

DECIPHERING THE UNKNOWN: DEALINGS IN DOCUMENTARIES

1. 16mm film facilitated mobility for the camera without affecting picture quality. It could be loaded onto a camera and the camera hefted onto someone's shoulder and carried around.
2. Newsreels are often 'staged' re-enactments of events that had already happened. The intention is not to interfere with events as they are in the process of happening. Much of the footage from the early twentieth-century wars, for instance, was staged; the cameramen would usually re-enact and film a battle scene at the site where the original action took place.
3. A city symphony is a documentary film without any characters or plot. The genre emerged in several countries simultaneously and lasted only for a decade spanning the 1920s. The name comes from the fact that they were devised along the structural and formal lines of an orchestra symphony. They used camera angles, the juxtaposition of shots, or editing techniques to emphasise certain scenes or details, the height of buildings, the enormous crowds boarding or alighting from a train, or the moving wheels and pistons in factories; or to create rapid transitions to show contrasts.
4. J. G. Ballard, author of *The atrocity exhibition*, in an interview with film historian, Mark Goodall, in Vertigo magazine. Retrieved from https://www.closeupfilmcentre.com/vertigo_magazine/volume-3-issue-9-spring-summer-2008/
5. Some important early documentary makers Dharamsey Bhai mentions are Kantilal Rathod (*Kanku, 1970*), Rajbans

Khanna *(Gautama the Buddha, The story of kashmir,* and *The rivers will not forget),* Govind Saraiyya *(Indian Coins)* and Satyadeva Dube *(Aparichayake Vindhyachal).* Taken from *Interview with Dharamsey Bhai: Independent Film Historian, as given to Dr Camille Deprez (2015)* and printed in, Cinematic Realism: Documentary Film Website, Hongkong Baptist University Library. Retrieved from https://digital.lib.hkbu.edu.hk/documentary-film/dharamsey.php

6 *Nine Months to Freedom*, on the Bangladesh Liberation War, was perhaps the first documentary to secure a theatrical release in India.

7 S.N.S. Sastry belonged to the Films Division, having joined it as a newsreel cameraman in the 1950s. However, Sastry went on to become a renowned filmmaker in his own right, with a distinct voice and style. Biography of S.N.S Sastry, The Movie DB. Retrieved from https://www.themoviedb.org/person/1469454-s-n-s-sastry

8 Bhownagary's documentary, *Radha Krishna*, was a wonderful short film on Kangra miniature paintings.

9 See Hong Kong Baptist University Library (2015) *Cinematic realism,* Documentary Film Website. Retrieved from http://digital.lib.hkbu.edu.hk/documentary-film/ [Accessed on 27 August]

10 Chatterjee, Saibal (2003) *Censoring documentaries* [Online] Hindustan Times. Retrieved from https://www.hindustantimes.com/india/censoring-documentaries/story-kJvzFA9U02vzKst8eoywdM.html

11 Juxtaposition is an editing technique in which the scenes being juxtaposed are unrelated to the meaning being

conveyed. Sometimes scenes are juxtaposed in a different chronological order to the events in the film.

12 Shedde, Meenakshi (2017) *New Trends in the Indian Documentary.* Azim Premji University Colloquium Series. Retrieved from https://www.youtube.com/watch?v=cUjwLTXBBzA

13 Hybrid documentaries use a mix of different tools like home videos, music, comedy, or animation to construct deliberate creative interventions.

14 Nishit Saran's parents set up the Nishit Saran Foundation after his death. Minna's recollections and Nishit's writings are posted on the Foundation's Website.

15 Wangchuk, R.N (2020) *Last of the Himalayan Honey Hunters: The Amazing Craft of a Brave Arunachal Tribe.* Retrieved from https://www.thebetterindia.com/225767/arunachal-pradesh-last-honey-hunters-chi-lupo-kezang-thongdok-award-winning-documentary-india-nor41/

16 Debord, Guy; Wolman, Gil (1956) *A user's guide to detournement* [Online] Bureau of Public Secrets. Retrieved from http://www.bopsecrets.org/SI/detourn.htm

17 *Bill Viola's Art of Immediacy* (2017) University of Westminster [Online] Retrieved from https://filmtvmovingimage.wordpress.com/2017/03/01/bill-violas-art-of-immediacy/

18 For example, *Signs that say what you want them to say and not signs that say what someone else wants you to say* (1992–93). Retrieved from https://www.artsy.net/artist/gillian-wearing

19 Wong, Ming (2014) *Installation view: bülent wongsoy: Biji diva!* [Online] Retrieved from http://www.mingwong.org/installation-view-bulent-wongsoy-biji-diva

20 Grierson, John (1971) A Movement is founded – first principles of documentary. In: Forsyth Hardy (ed.)(1971) *Grierson on Documentary.* Berkely and Los Angeles : University of California Press. P.147.

PAINTING GANDHI ON THE CELLULOID CANVAS: A STUDENT ESSAY

1   Varma, Sujata (2016) *Gandhi memorials pan India to go digital* [Online] The Hindu. Retrieved from https://www.thehindu.com/news/national/telangana/Gandhi-memorials-pan-India-to-go-digital/article16802119.ece

2   All this information and more is available in a book, *In the tracks of the Mahatma: The making of a documentary*, by A. K. Chettiar, edited and introduced by A. R. Venkatachelapathy, translated from Tamil by S. Thillainayagam, and published by Orient Blackswan, Pvt. Ltd., 2007. Other documentaries on Gandhi include *Gandhi: The 20th Century Prophet* (available in parts on YouTube, the Gandhi Heritage Portal), and *Mahatma – Life of Gandhi 1869 –1948* which is a 5 hour 9-minute documentary by Vithalbhai Jhaveri (1968), available on http://guides.library.cornell.edu/gandhi/films

3   First published by Jonathan Cape in London in 1951; published in India by Bhartiya Vidya Bhavan, K. M. Munshi Marge, Mumbai 400 007.

4   *Gandhi* won a total of eight Oscars from the eleven nominations it received by the Academy.

5   'I had not shared my thoughts with my wife until then, but only consulted her at the time of taking the vow. She had no objection...Before the vow, I had been open to being overcome

by temptation at any moment. Now the vow was a sure shield against temptation', he wrote. *Brahmacharya-II*. Retrieved from https://www.mkgandhi.org/autobio/chap62.htm

6   Gandhi's followers are believed to have objected to this scene as they found it incredible that Gandhi and Ba would publicly share such intimate moments.

7   She also writes in a similar vein, 'बापू ने मुझसे कहा कि अगर मैं इस प्रयोग में बेदाग निकल आई तो मेरा चरित्र आसमान चूमने लगेगा, मुझे जीवन में एक बड़ा सबक मिलेगा और मेरे सिर पर मंडराते विवादों के सारे बादल छंट जाएंगे. बापू का कहना था कि यह उनके ब्रह्मचर्य का यज्ञ है और मैं उसका पवित्र हिस्सा हूं. उन्होंने कहा कि ईश्वर से यही प्रार्थना है कि उन्हें शुद्ध रखे, उन्हें सत्य का साथ देने की शक्ति दे और निर्भय बनाए. उन्होंने मुझसे कहा कि अगर सब हमारा साथ छोड़ जाएं, तब भी ईश्वर के आशीर्वाद से हम यह प्रयोग सफलतापूर्वक करेंगे और फिर इस महापरीक्षा के बारे में सारी दुनिया को बताएंगे.' - Excerpts from Manu's diaries. Mahurkar, Uday (2013) *Mahatma and Manuben* [Online] Retrieved from http://swaadheen.blogspot.com/2015/07/mahatma-and-manuben.html

8   Gandhi, M.K (12 May 1920) *Young India*.p. 2.

9   Gandhi, M.K (5 September 1936) *Harijan*.

10 Gandhi, M.K (28 May 1924) *Young India*.

11 Gandhi, M.K (27 February 1930) *Young India*.

12 The 'Dandi March' as it is popularly called, was a demonstration carried out by Gandhi and his followers in 1930, against the British tax on salt. Gandhi walked almost 400 miles from Ahmedabad to the sea near Dandi with hundreds of his countrymen, in order to show the British that Indians could make salt for themselves.

13 Sethi, Sunil (1980) *Behind the scenes of Richard*

Attenborough's Gandhi. [Online] India Today. Retrieved from https://www.indiatoday.in/magazine/cover-story/story/19801231-behind-the-scenes-of-richard-attenborough-gandhi-773679-2013-11-29

14 Brook, Tom (2014) *What is the secret of a good biopic? [Online] BBC*. Retrieved from https://www.bbc.com/culture/article/20140728-what-makes-a-good-biopic

15 Nandy, Pritish (2000) *Gandhi pushed Ambedkar to the edge.* Retrieved from https://www.rediff.com/entertai/2000/jun/27jabb.htm

16 Gandhi, M.K (1926) *Young India*. Ahmedabad.

17 Speech to Indian labourers in the coolie barracks of Rangoon, Burma; 10 March 1929.

18 Gandhi, M.K. (2015) *An Autobiography: The Story of My Experiments with Truth*. Ahmedabad: Navjivan Publication House.